mustsees
BARCELONA

Detail of La Sagrada Família ©markz/Dreamstime.com

MICHELIN

General Manager	Cynthia Clayton Ochterbeck

mustsees **Barcelona**

Editorial Manager	Jonathan P. Gilbert
Editorial	JMS Books, Jo Murray
Author	Jenni Davis
Contributing Writers	Charlotte Hurdman, Alan Moore,
	Jane Moseley, Jackie Strachan
Production Manager	Natasha G. George
Cartography	Stephane Anton, John Dear, Thierry Lemasson
Photo Editor	Yoshimi Kanazawa
Photo Researcher	Emma O'Neill
Layout	Chris Bell, cbdesign, Satzomatic
Cover & Interior Design	Chris Bell, cbdesign

Contact Us	Michelin Maps and Guides
	One Parkway South
	Greenville, SC 29615
	USA
	www.michelintravel.com
	Michelin Maps and Guides
	Hannay House
	39 Clarendon Road
	Watford, Herts WD17 1JA
	UK
	☎ (01923) 205 240
	www.ViaMichelin.com
	travelpubsales@uk.michelin.com

Special Sales	For information regarding bulk sales, customized
	editions and premium sales, please contact
	our Customer Service Departments:
	USA 1-800-432-6277
	UK (01923) 205 240
	Canada 1-800-361-8236

Michelin Apa Publications Ltd
A joint venture between Michelin and Langenscheidt

58 Borough High Street, London SE1 1XF, United Kingdom

No part of this publication may be reproduced in any form
without the prior permission of the publisher.

© 2010 Michelin Apa Publications Ltd
ISBN 978-1-907099-00-7
Printed: August 2010
Printed and bound: Himmer, Germany

Note to the reader:
While every effort is made to ensure that all information printed in this guide is correct and
up-to-date, Michelin Apa Publications Ltd. accepts no liability for any direct, indirect or
consequential losses howsoever caused so far as such can be excluded by law. Admission
prices listed for sights in this guide are for a single adult, unless otherwise specified.

Welcome to Barcelona

Hospital de Sant Pau

p 20

©Gregory Wrona/APA Publications

Introduction

p 28

R. Mattes/MICHELIN

TABLE OF CONTENTS

p 98

J. Malburet/Michelin

TABLE OF CONTENTS

★★★ ATTRACTIONS

Unmissable historic and cultural sights

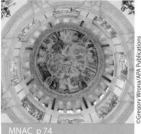
©Gregory Wrona/APA Publications

MNAC p 74

©Yvon52/Dreamstime.com

©Val Bakhtin/Dreamstime.com

La Sagrada Família p 64

Sant Pere de Rodes p 100

Ph. Robic/Michelin

Parc Güell p 66

Casa Milà p 62

Yury Zaporozhchenko/Dreamstime.com

Plaça Reial p 27

©Bcollet/Dreamstime.com

Catedral Santa Eulàlia p 30

©Patrick Poendl/Dreamstime.com

Casa Batlló p 60

© Rob Broek/iStockphoto.com

STAR ATTRACTIONS

STAR ATTRACTIONS

Unmissable historic, cultural, and natural sights

For more than 75 years people have used Michelin stars to take the guesswork out of travel. Our star-rating system helps you make the best decision on where to go, what to do, and what to see.

★★★	Unmissable
★★	Worth a trip
★	Worth a detour
No star	recommended

Looking out the window of Casa Batlló

©Gregory Wrona/APA Publications

ACTIVITIES

Unmissable entertainment, activities, and restaurants.

Outings

Follow the Modernisme Route *p73*

Get a bird's eye view from the Collserola Tower *p58*

Have fun at the Sant Joan Festival *p10*

See a performance at the Festival del Grec *p10*

Visit the extraordinary Sagrada Família *p64*

Kids

Be a chocoholic at the Museu de la Xocolata *p119*

Explore a rainforest at CosmoCaixa – Museu de la Ciència *p118*

Walk through the middle of the ocean at L'Aquàrium *p116*

Sports

Watch a basketball game *p112*

Learn about the Barca legend at the FCB museum *p114*

Explore the city by bicycle *p112*

See *castellers* build a human tower *p113*

Food/Drink

Try tapas at Cal Pep *p146*

Cakes at the legendary Café Zurich *p144*

Sample Catalan dishes at Cinc Sentis *p138*

Shopping

Visit the oldest shop in Barcelona *p130*

Home deco heaven, Vinçon *p130*

Hunt antiques in the Barri Gòtic *p130*

Snap up a bargain at Els Encants Vells *p132*

Hotels

See Gaudi's influence at Hotel Majestic *p154*

Relax on the rooftop patio at the Hotel Pulitzer *p149*

Nightlife

See a concert at Palau de la Música Catalana *p120*

Sip a drink as the sun sets at La Caseta del Migdia, Montjuïc *p124*

See a show at Tablao Flamenco Cordobés *p121*

See Catalan folk traditions *p121*

STAR ATTRACTIONS

Listed below are just some of the city's most popular annual events.

January

Cavalcada de Reis
Epiphany. The Three Kings parade through the city *(Jan 5)*

February

Santa Eulàlia
Co-patron saint with St Jordi, she is honored with parades and concerts *(around Feb 12)*

Carnaval
King Carnestoltes leads a procession through the streets; masked balls, eating, drinking, and other festivities *(end Feb)*

March

Festes de Sant Medir
A parade through Gràcia in costume with horse-drawn carriages, fireworks to end *(Mar 3)*

Castellers at the Festes de la Mercè

April

Dia de Sant Jordi
Men and women exchange books and roses on St George's Day *(Apr 23)*

Feria de Abril
Festival atmosphere with dancing and concerts *(end Apr/early May)*

May

Fira de Sant Ponç
C. de l'Hospital. A fair selling herbs, honey, and other natural products *(May 11)*

Flamenco Festival
The best *cantaores* and guitarists at venues across the city *(end May)*

June

L'Ou Com Balla
Corpus Christi. "Dancing" eggs bob about on some of the city's fountains *(first half Jun)*

Festival de Sónar
Very popular three-day electronic and multimedia music festival *(mid-Jun)*

Festa de la Música
Free music events throughout the city *(Jun 21)*

Revetila de Sant Joan
Fireworks, fun, food, and cava at the beach *(Jun 23 evening)*

Festival del Grec
An arts festival at venues all over the city, including the open-air Teatre Grec on Montjuïc *(see p 121, end Jun–early Aug)*

July

Music in the Parks
Concerts in parks *(Thu, Fri, Sat through Jul)*

©Turespaña

MUST KNOW

April: *Feria de Abril*

© Rafael Campillo/Pictures Colour Library

August

Festa Major de Gràcia
A number of the city's districts hold a *festa major* with six days of celebrations; this is one of the best *(mid-Aug)*

Festa de Sant Roc
Barri Gòtic—traditional parades, street games, *sardana (see p 121)*, and fireworks *(mid-Aug)*

September

Diada Nacional de Catalunya
Patriotic flag-waving and parades on Catalan National Day *(Sept 11)*

Festes de la Mercè
Barcelona celebrates its patron saint (Santa Eulàlia, also known as Our Lady of Mercy) with traditional Catalan activities, music, fireworks *(around Sept 24)*

October

Festival de Musiques del Món
World music festival with a program of concerts featuring artists from all over the world

La Castanyada
All Saints Day. Roast Chestnuts *(castanyes)* and other traditional food treats *(Oct 31–Nov 1)*

December

Fira de Santa Llúcia
Pl. de la Seu. Christmas fair selling traditional decorations, including the famous *caganers* *(Dec 1–24)*

> **A saint in common**
> Catalonia and England (along with a number of other countries) have something in common when it comes to patron saints, they both share St George (Jordi), although in Barcelona it is the red and gold Catalan flag that is hung everywhere on April 23, rather than the simple red cross of St George. On this day Catalan men give women a red rose, while women reciprocate with a book.

11

PRACTICAL INFORMATION

WHEN TO GO

Barcelona is busiest in the summer months when visitors fill the city, but this is not the best time to go. In August, many shops, bars, and restaurants close as locals leave to escape the heat and humidity. The best time to visit is late spring and early fall, when temperatures are mild – although heavy downpours are common in October. Crisp, cool sunny days are normal in winter, and snow is rare. Barcelona has more festivals than weeks of the year, but the key celebration is September's Festes de la Mercè, when the city is especially lively.

KNOW BEFORE YOU GO

There are many sources of information to help you plan your trip.

Useful websites

www.barcelonaturisme.com – Excellent official website of the Barcelona tourist board.
www.bcn.es – In-depth information provided by Barcelona city authority.
www.timeout.com/barcelona – One of the best guides to what's on in Barcelona.
www.spain.info – The Spanish tourist board's website has an impressive section on Barcelona.
www.barcelonayellow.com – Regularly updated comprehensive information about the city.

Other websites worth a look:
www.myft.net
www.barcelona-online.com

Tourist information

Turisme de Barcelona – Plaça de Catalunya 17, 08026 Barcelona. ℰ(0034) 93 285 38 34; www.barcelonaturisme.com. The tourist office is under-ground—look for large pillars with an "I" on top near the El Corte Inglés department store.

International visitors

Australian Consulate:
ℰ93 490 90 13. www.spain.embassy.gov.au.
Canadian Consulate:
ℰ93 412 72 36. www.canada international.gc.ca/spain-espagne/index.aspx?lang=eng.
Irish Consulate:
ℰ93 491 50 21. www.irlanda.es/home/index.aspx.
New Zealand Consulate:
ℰ93 209 03 99. www.nzembassy.com/spain.
UK Consulate:
ℰ93 366 62 00. http://ukinspain.fco.gov.uk/en.
US Consulate:
ℰ93 280 22 27; (emergencies ℰ91 587 22 00). www.embusa.es/barcelonaen.html.

Entry requirements

Passports – A valid passport is required by everyone entering Spain, except nationals of European Union countries covered by the Schengen Agreement, who need only an official ID card. The UK and Republic of Ireland are not signatories to this agreement, so citizens of these countries need passports. Loss or theft of your passport should be reported to the embassy and the local police.

Barcelona average seasonal temperatures				
	Jan	Apr	Jul	Oct
Avg. High	13°C/55°F	17°C/62°F	27°C/81°F	21°C/70°F
Avg. Low	4°C/40°F	8°C/47°F	19°C/66°F	12°C/54°F

Visas – Visas are not required for nationals of the US, Canada, Australia, and New Zealand who are visiting Spain for less than three months. Citizens of South Africa and other countries need visas to enter Spain. Apply to your nearest Spanish consulate before you travel. For up-to-date information, visit the Spanish Ministry of Foreign Affairs website: www.maec.es.

Customs Regulations

For EU citizens there are no limits to what you can buy and take with you, provided it is for your own personal use. There are recommended allowances for alcohol and tobacco, however; and you must declare cash in excess of €6,000.

US citizens can check the Department of State's website (travel.state.gov) for information on international travel. Download the US Customs and Border Protection's publication, *Know Before You Go* at www.cbp.gov.

GETTING THERE
By Air

The quickest and easiest way to reach Barcelona is to fly direct to the El Prat de Llobregat airport.

Barcelona Airport – ✆ 90 240 47 04. www.aena.es. 7mi/12km south of Barcelona on the C-31 Barcelona–Castelldefels road. For details on how to get to and from the city centre, go to the Aeropuertos Espanoles y Navegacion Aerea website (www.aena.es); choose Barcelona Airport; then "practical information." Other airports near Barcelona include Girona and Reus; both are over an hour away from the city.

Girona Airport – ✆ 97 218 67 08. www.barcelona-girona-airport. com. 65mi/103km northeast of Barcelona via the AP7 toll road.

Important Numbers	
Emergency *(Catalonia; 24hrs)*	112
Policia Nacional (National Police)	091
Guardia Urbana (Local Police; for traffic and minor crimes)	092
Mossos d''Esquadra (Catalan Police)	088
Guardia Civil	062
Medical Emergencies	061
Fire Service	080

Reus Airport – ☎ 97 777 22 04. www.reus-airport.es. 66mi/106km southwest of Barcelona via the A-7 motorway.

By Ship
Ferries from the Balearic Islands and main Mediterranean ports dock at Estació Marítima, a short walk from Plaça Portal de la Pau at the bottom of La Rambla (the nearest metro is Drassanes).

By Train
The city's main railway station is Sants Estació. It is the terminus for the High-Speed Train (AVE) and many national and international services, as well as trains to Barcelona Airport. Estació de Franca handles long-distance intercity services from Madrid, Seville, Malaga, and other major cities, as well as international services from Paris, Zurich, Milan, and Geneva. Some trains stop at both Sants and Franca. For schedules and fares: www.renfe.com; ☎ 90 224 02 02.

By Bus
The main bus terminal is the Estació del Nord on Avda Vilanova (main entrance at Ali-bei 80; nearest metro Arc de Triomf). Some intercity and international services also leave from the smaller terminal next to Sants railway station at Plaça Joan Peiro. For information and ticket times, see www.barcelonanord.com; or call ☎ 90 226 06 06 or ☎ 90 230 32 22. For European bus travel, visit www.eurolines.com.

By Car
Barcelona lies just 93mi/150km from the French border and is well linked to the rest of Europe and Spain by a number of fast *autopistes* (motorways). Coming into Barcelona on any one of the highways, head for the Ronda Litoral, the southern half of the city's ring road. Follow signs for the Port toward the main exit for old town (Port Vell).
For more information, visit www.idealspain.com/pages/information/DrivingSpain.htm or www.autopistas.com.
Motorways in Spain are often subject to tolls (*peajes*).

GETTING AROUND
Barcelona is extremely compact and most areas are best explored on foot. Tourist offices provide free street maps; there is an excellent interactive street map at www.bcn.cat/guia.

Public Transportation
Barcelona has a very good public transport system, which, despite being run by different organizations, is highly integrated. A single fare on the metro or bus costs €1.40, but a more economical ticket (*targeta*) is the ten-trip T-10 for €7.95, which can be shared by up to ten people. The T-10 is valid for 75 minutes from the moment it is first stamped with the date and time in a ticket-validation machine. Within those 75 minutes, you can combine any bus, tram, and suburban railway trip with one metro journey. It is also valid on the Tramvía Blau (blue tram), the Montjuïc Funicular, and the RENFE train to the airport—but not on the Aerobus (the express bus service to the airport). You can buy T-10s at news stands as well as on the metro and train systems

(from machines or the ticket office), but not on buses. There are many other integrated ticket options available, including day passes that provide unlimited travel on public transport. For details, ee the website of Transports Metropolitans de Barcelona (TMB) (www.tmb.cat) or call ☎ 93 318 70 74.

A worthwhile investment, the **Barcelona Card** includes unlimited use of public transport within zone 1. For information, visit www.barcelonaturisme.com.

By Bus

Barcelona has a fleet of more than 1,000 buses that operate on over 80 routes, covering the entire city. Bus stops are clearly marked and buses post their destinations on the front. Buses are adapted for people with reduced mobility. Most services operate from 4:25am–11pm and run every 10–15 minutes (less frequently on weekends).

Tickets bought from bus drivers don't allow transfers. For further information visit www.tmb.cat or call ☎ 93 318 71 74.

Night buses (*nitbus*) operate from 11pm–6am. They all stop at or depart from Plaça de Catalunya. For tickets, routes and prices, visit www.emt-amb.com (in Spanish). There are many open-air **tour buses**, but the white and turquoise Barcelona Bus Turístic is run by the city's public transport authority, and all their buses have wheelchair access. This tour bus has 44 stops along three routes. You can hop on and off as many times as you like along the journey; the ticket is valid on all three routes. A one-day ticket costs €22 (€14 for children 4-12). See www.barcelonabusturistic.cat for more information.

By Rail

Ferrocarrils de la Generalitat de Catalunya (FGC) is the city's commuter rail system. It runs on three lines and shares key stations – and similar prices and hours – with the metro. FGC stations and trains are marked with a reclining S-like blue-and-white icon. Information and tickets: www.fgc.net/eng/barcelona-valles.asp; ☎ 93 205 15 15.

By Metro

The quickest way of getting around Barcelona is by metro, which operates on six color-coded lines. Entrances are marked by red diamond signs. Metro trains run 5am–midnight and until 2am on Fri. A non-stop service operates on Saturdays and major fiestas. Download a map of the metro from www.tmb.cat.

By Taxi

Barcelona's 11,000 taxis are easily identified by their yellow and black livery, and It is easy to hail them on the street. A green light on the roof indicates the taxi is available for hire. There is also a taxi service for people with reduced mobility (book in advance at Taxi Amic, ☎ 93 420 80 88). Supplemental fees apply to luggage, journeys to and from the airport, and travel after midnight and on Sundays and holidays. For further information, see the Institut Metropolita del Taxi website (www.taxibarcelona.cat) or call ☎ 93 223 51 51.

By Tram

Barcelona's newest form of transport operates on two lines: the Trambaix and the Trambesós. All trams are fully accessible for wheelchair users and are part of the integrated ticket system. They run 5am–midnight and until 2pm Fri, Sat, and the eve of public holidays. Go to www.trambcn. com for more information. The last vestige of Barcelona's original tram system, the Tramvia Blau (Blue Tram; www.barcelonabusturistic. cat/web/guest/tramviablau), is now a tourist attraction and a pleasant way to reach Tibidabo hill.

By Funicular & Cable Car

Integrated into the metro network is the Montjuïc Funicular, a cog railroad that connects Paral·lel metro to the hill of Montjuïc. A *telefèric* (cable car) then takes you up to Montjuïc Castle (winter 10am–6pm; summer 10am–9pm). The fare is €6.30 one-way (round-trip €9; children age 4-12 one-way €4.80, round-trip €6.50). Another cable car, the Transbordador Aeri del Port, runs from Montjuïc across the harbor to Torre de Jaume I, on Barcelona's *moll* (quay), and on to Torre de Sant Sebastià in Barceloneta. You can board at either stage (fare is €12.50 round-trip; €9 one way; winter noon–5:30pm, summer 10:30–8pm).

To reach the summit of Tibidabo hill, take the metro to Avinguda de Tibidabo, then the Tramvía Blau (fare is €2.80 one-way, €4.30 round-trip) to Peu del Funicular, and finally the Tibidabo Funicular (€4 round-trip) from there to the Tibidabo amusement park. The Tibidabo Funicular runs every 30 minutes, (7:05am–9:35pm ascending; 7:25am–9:55pm descending).

By Boat

Barcelona is a city that loves the sea, and traditional leisure cruisers – called Las Golondrinas – ply the waters of the port. A tour of the harbor takes 35 minutes, while a tour on a larger sea-going catamaran from the Columbus Monument to Bogatell Beach and the Olympic Harbor takes 2 hours. For more information, call ℰ 93 442 31 06 or visit www.lasgolondrinas.com.

By Bike

The city authority is very keen to promote cycling and there are over 62mi/100km of cycle lanes (*carrils bici*) along major avenues throughout the city and the seafront. You can also cycle through the area's open spaces and parks. See the city authority's website (www.bcn.es/bicicleta/en/bici_carrils.html) for information about where to hire a bike. Cycle lane maps can be picked up from tourist offices and rental shops or downloaded from the website.

By Car

Getting around Barcelona by car is generally more trouble than it's worth. The *rondas* (ring roads) make entering and exiting the city easy (unless it's rush hour), but parking, navigating and police patrols make driving a hassle. If you must use your car, Barcelona has a large number of car parks, many located in the city centre. Charges range from €2–3 an hour to around €35 per day. On-street parking is complicated, and the police are quick to hand out tickets or tow cars away. Some streets have time-controlled, pop-up bollards, meaning you may get stuck. Never park in front of doors marked "Gual Permanent," where 24hr-access is needed.

By GoCar

GoCars are yellow three-wheel vehicles fitted with a GPS system that provides a virtual guide to the city's sights. There are two routes, uptown and downtown, or you can plan your own route if you prefer. GoCar rates range from €29 for an hour to €99 for a whole day. Book by phone, online, or at their base next to Santa Caterina market (C. Freixures 23 bis bajos; 📞93 269 17 92; www.gocartours. es/reservations-bcn@gocartours. com). You need to be over 21 with a valid driver's licence.

BASIC INFORMATION
Accessibility

Barcelona is working hard to improve facilities for the disabled. Many buses have been adapted for people with reduced mobility, while more than half the metro stations have accessible lifts, ticket machines and barriers, as well as guides for the visually impaired. The tram network is fully accessible for the disabled, as are most of the city's museums and cultural venues, parks and tourist attractions. Special minibus taxis adapted for wheelchairs can be ordered from Taxi Amic (see Taxis). Websites with comprehensive information on access to venues and transport around the city include: www.bcn.es/accessible; the Accessible Barcelona Guide, www.vienaeditorial.com/ barcelonaaccesible; and www.aspace.cat/aspacet/turisme.

Accommodations

Barcelona has a range of places to stay, from youth hostels and campsites to apartments and boutique hotels. *See Must Stay* for a list of suggested hotels.

Reservations services
Hotels
- You can book a hotel through the Barcelona tourist board's website: www.barcelona turisme.cat/Where-to-sleep. They also have lists of youth hostels, apartments and campsites.

Bed and breakfast
- www.bedandbreakfast.com/ barcelona-spain.html.

Youth hostels
- www.hostelworld.com; www.youthostel.com.

Business hours

Stores are usually open Mon–Sat 9 or 10am to 1 or 2pm, and then from 4 or 5 pm to 8 or 9pm. Many smaller businesses don't reopen on Saturday afternoons. Department stores don't close at lunchtime. In August, many shops, bars, restaurants, and even some sights are closed as the locals are on holiday. Many museums are closed on Monday.

Banks are open 8am–2pm, Mon–Fri. Some are also open 4pm–8pm Thu and 8am–2pm Sat, except from July–September.

Post offices (*correus*) are usually open 8:30am–8pm, Mon–Fri and 10am–1pm Sat.

Communications

Public phones (*cabines*) take coins, phone cards and credit cards. Phone centers (*locutoris*) are more comfortable and usually cheaper than public pay phones. For less expensive international calls, purchase a **calling card** (€6) from a newsstand, phone center, or tobacconist (*estanc*). The cards have a toll-free number you can call from any phone.

Cell phones (*móvil*) in Spain use the European standard GSM networks. Not all US or Canadian cell phones are GSM-compatible; check with your provider before leaving home.

Area codes – Barcelona phone numbers all begin with 93.

To make an international call from Barcelona, dial 00, followed by the country code (UK 44; US/Canada 1; Australia 61; New Zealand 64), the area code, and the phone number. To call Spain from abroad, dial the international access code, then 34 for Spain, plus the phone number.

Discounts

If you plan to visit many museums, consider purchasing a pass, available from the Barcelona tourist office and the venues themselves. The **Barcelona Card** (good for 2–5 consecutive days) offers up to 50 percent off admission to the city's main attractions, plus free travel on public transport.

Articket, valid for six months, provides free entry to seven museums. **ARQUEOticket**, valid for a year, includes entry to five museums ide Barcelona.

For details, check online at www.barcelonaturisme.com. The tourist office can provide a list of all the free museum days. Most museums also offer a 30-50 percent discount for people over 65.

Electricity

Throughout Spain, the electricity supply is 220 volts/50 Hz, using two-pin wall sockets. Buy adapters and converters before leaving home. Some North American 110-volt appliances will also need a transformer—without it your appliance may be ruined.

Health

Before leaving, check your personal insurance to see if it covers you abroad. Visitors can receive emergency care through the public Servei Catalá de la Salut. EU citizens are entitled to free basic medical care with a European Health Insurance Card (obtain one before traveling). Citizens of some other countries, notably South America, also have access to free care.

All travelers are strongly advised to take out additional medical coverage. If you are taking medications, bring your prescriptions when traveling. Visitors will find 24-hour emergency rooms (*urgències*) at: Centre d'Urgències Perecamps (Avda Drassanes 13-15; ✆93 441 06 00; metro: Drassanes or Paral·lel); Hospital de la Santa Creu I de Sant Pau (c/Sant Antoni Maria Claret 167; ✆93 291 90 00; metro: San Pau); and Hospital Clinic I Provincial (c/Villaroel 170; ✆93 227 54 00; metro: Hospital Clinic).

Drug Stores (*farmàcies; open 9am–2pm and 4:30pm–8pm*) are marked by a green cross. One drug store per neighborhood is open all night on a rotating basis—check with the individual farmàcia. For further information, see www.farmaceuticonline.com. Barcelona has numerous dental clinics, including Clínica Dental Barcelona *(Mon–Fri 9am–midnight)*.

Internet

There are Internet centers all over Barcelona. Most libraries have free Internet points and wireless access for public use—but you might have to join the library first. The city council is seting up free Wi-Fi access in 500 public spaces.

Money and Currency exchange

The unit of currency is the euro, which is divided into 100 *céntims*, or cents. Notes are issued in €5, €10, €20, €50, €100, €200, and €500 denominations and coins in 1, 2, 5, 10, 20 and 50 cents, and €1 and €2. Payment by debit card, Visa or Mastercard is widespread. American Express and Diner's Card are less widely accepted. Money may be withdrawn from a bank or an ATM *(bancomat)*; credit cards will charge a transaction fee. Bring a photo ID when making a credit-card purchase in a shop. If your card is lost or stolen, call the police and the credit-card company. Money can be changed in post offices, banks, currency-exchange offices *(cambios)*, and at railway stations and the airport; take your passport as ID.

Post offices

See Business Hours. Barcelona's main post office at Plaça Antonio López is open longer hours. *Poste restante (Lista de correus)* letters arrive here; bring your passport to claim your mail. Bright yellow mailboxes often have one slot

for *ciutat* (city) and one for *altres destinacions* (other destinations). Stamps are easy to buy at *estancs*.

Public holidays

Not all holidays in Spain are observed in Catalonia and vice versa. The following are public holidays in Barcelona: New Year's Day (Jan 1), Epiphany (Jan 6), Good Friday, Easter Sunday, Easter Monday, Labor Day (May 1), Whit Monday (50 days after Easter), Dia de Sant Joan (Jun 24), Assumption (Aug 15), La Diada (Catalan Independence Day; Sept 11), Festes de la Mercè (Sept 24), National Day (Oct 12), All Saints' Day (Nov 1), Constitution Day (Dec 6), Immaculate Conception (Dec 8), Christmas Day (Dec 25), and St. Stephen's Day (Dec 26).

Smoking

As of June 2010, Spain has joined the rest of Europe by banning smoking in all public places, including restaurants and cafés.

Taxes and Tipping

Non-EU citizens can claim an IVA (sales tax) refund on most purchases over €90 when they leave Spain. Shops displaying the tax-free logo will provide a tax-refundable receipt, which you present before check-in at the airport. IVA of 16 percent is included in the advertised price. For hotels, the 7-percent IVA is not always included in the rate. Tipping is not the norm in Spain. In restaurants, diners tip about 5 percent of the bill; if you're eating a light meal, round up the bill to the nearest 50 cents. Taxi drivers are usually tipped 5 percent, and hotel porters about 50 cents per bag.

WELCOME TO BARCELONA

The first thing to remember when you visit Barcelona is that you're not merely in a city in Spain—rather, you're in the capital of Catalonia, a distinction of which the Barcelonans are extremely mindful. Catalan identity—hard-fought and hard-won—manifests in all manner of ways, from architecture to art, from language to music and dance, from culture to cuisine… and perhaps it is this that makes Barcelona so attractive to the millions of people who flock to experience it. Indeed, it's Europe's fourth most-visited city, which is quite an achievement when you consider that it's competing with the giants—Paris, London, and Rome.

In Barcelona, centuries and styles coexist and overlap. Barcelona was founded in the 3C BC by Hannibal's father, Hamilcar Barca, and named Barcino after his family. The layout followed the typical Roman grid pattern, which later served as the foundation for the expanding medieval city. The Barri Gòtic and La Ribera bear witness to the proud maritime city that once ruled the Mediterranean, while the narrow alleys seem unchanged since Gothic times.

So what's it all about in the here and now? Here's a hint of what it has to offer. Barcelona is compact and exciting, a party city that never sleeps—it comes alive at night, and conventional hours simply don't exist here. It's a chameleon that knows how

to move with the times, yet has that long history at its core. With its atmospheric medieval center and contemporary, daring, even eccentric architecture, Barca caters for every tourist and taste. Whatever you are looking for, this city has it. History, art, architecture, churches, museums, theater, cinema, gastronomy, sports, parks, even beaches—no problem. Restaurants serving regional food, tasty tapas, and the latest in international cuisine and *nueva cocina*? Barcelona is your oyster. Atmospheric squares in which to relax over a glass of red wine and watch the world go by? Tick. Courtyards and cloisters so tranquil it hardly seems possible? They're tucked away all over the city, just waiting for you to

Parc Güell

INTRODUCTION

stumble upon them. Do you feel like traditional Catalan dances and sounds on a warm night or showing the locals your latest moves to the coolest grooves in the hottest clubs? Look no farther. How about a shop-till-you-drop morning in unique boutiques? Bring your list. Or just a chill on the beach? Pack your swimming gear. Versatile and vibrant, dynamic and daring, Barcelona is a perfect destination for all: single travelers, romantic couples, families with children, lovers of art and architecture, gourmets and wine buffs, football fans, and sports enthusiasts.

When you arrive in the city, you will find yourself almost inexorably drawn to La Rambla, a long avenue that epitomizes the spirit of Barcelona. Take time to stroll from one end to the other, admiring the buildings, wandering among the market stalls, being entertained by the buskers and human statues vying for your attention, and—most importantly—pausing when the mood takes you to sit with a drink on a café terrace and watch other people doing the same. When you feel you've started to understand what it's all about, it's time to start exploring farther afield.

If you want to continue simply wandering, head for the Barri Gòtic and get to know the historic heart of the city. Here you will find the cathedral, some magnificent squares, and any number of quirky little shops and cafés.

You might even be lucky enough to catch a spontaneous performance of *sardana*, the traditional Catalan dance. Go beyond the Barri Gòtic to La Ribera, and be wowed by the palatial buildings on Carrer de Montcada. When you've had your fill of being steeped in centuries of history, go to the other extreme and discover Modernisme— buildings erected in the late 19C and early 20C that take elements of the Catalan Gothic tradition and catapult them into the modern age. Time now for a little culture? The choices are endless—you can discover more about Barcelona's origins, or pore over collections of traditional Catalan art or the works of the exalted modern artists associated with the city. If you've come *en famille*, take the kids to the zoo, the aquarium, or the science museum, or acquaint them with the history of the city— in chocolate!

When early evening comes, head for a bar, order a glass of cava, and nibble on some tapas or *pintxos*. These miniature samples of local cuisine will keep you going until dinner. If you're used to eating early, it might take a few bouts of indigestion before you fall into step with the local custom of not dining until at least 9 o'clock! Tourist-oriented restaurants will feed you earlier—but when in Barcelona… Barcelona is also near some wonderful places to visit by rail or car. Escape for the day to Montserrat with its spectacular mountain views and monastery. Hop on a train to Sitges for a delicious lunch by the sea. You can even go from city center hustle and bustle to a beach bar in minutes within the city itself. Sun, sea, sand, shops, sightseeing, and some serious cultural and gourmet experiences await you in this intriguing place.

LA RAMBLA★★

Separating the Barri Gòtic and El Raval neighborhoods, La Rambla follows the course of a dry riverbed (Arabic: *al-ramla*) from the Plaça de Catalunya to the waterfront. Bustling with colorful life both day and night, this long, shady avenue is the place to experience the Barcelona vibe as you stroll among the stalls or relax at a sidewalk café, entertained by countless street performers.

🔊 WALKING TOUR

Start at the Plaça de Catalunya end of La Rambla and stroll down toward the sea, taking a few detours along the way to visit some of the sights tucked away on either side of the avenue.

Ⓜ *Catalunya (L1, L3), Liceu (L3), Drassanes (L3).*

✕ **Lunch stop** – La Boqueria/ Mercat de Sant Josep.

Rambla de Canaletes – La Rambla is actually a series of five ramblas. The first of these, Rambla de Canaletes, takes its name from the Font de Canaletes, a fountain, landmark, and popular meeting place. According to legend, visitors who drink from the fountain are destined to return to the city.

▶ *Turn left onto Santa Anna to visit Iglesia de Santa Anna.*

Santa Anna

Santa Anna 29. 93 301 35 76 . Open Mon–Sat 9am–1pm, 4.30–8.30pm, Sun and public holidays 9am–1pm.

Hidden away in a quiet, narrow street just off Rambla de Canaletes, this elegant Romanesque church was originally part of a monastery. The Gothic cloister, its pointed arches resting on slender columns, is particularly attractive.

▶ *Return to La Rambla, then cross over to C. Bonsuccès. Where the road bears right, continue on C. Elisabets to the C. dels Àngels. Turn right to Pl. dels Àngels to visit MACBA.*

La Rambla

© Gregory Wrona/Apa Publications

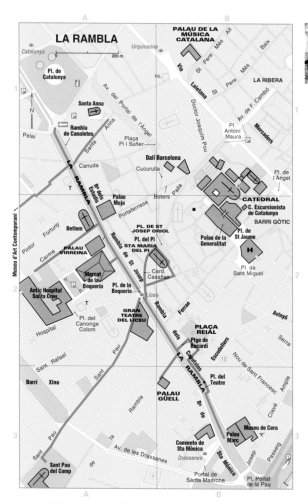

LA RAMBLA

Catalunya · Urquinaona

Pl. de Catalunya

Santa Anna

Rambla de Canaletes

Plaça Pi i Suñer

Dalí Barcelona

Cucurulla

Palau Moja

Portaferrissa

Betlem

PALAU VIRREINA

PL. DE ST JOSEP ORIOL

Pl. del Pi · STA MARIA DEL PI

Card. Casañas

Mercat de la Boqueria

Pl. de la Boqueria · Liceu

Antic Hospital Santa Creu

Pl. del Canonge Colom

GRAN TEATRE DEL LICEU

PLAÇA REIAL

Ptge de Bacardí

Barri Xino

PALAU GÜELL

Pl. del Teatre

Convento de Sta Mònica

Drassanes

Sant Pau del Camp

Av. de les Drassanes

Portal de Santa Madrona

Pl. Portal de la Pau

PALAU DE LA MÚSICA CATALANA

LA RIBERA

Pl. Antóni Maura

Mercaders

Pl. de l'Àngel

BARRI GÒTIC

CATEDRAL

C. Excursionista de Catalunya

Pl. de St Jaume

Palau de la Generalitat

Pl. de Sant Miquel

Avinyó

Palau Marc

Museu de Cera

Museu d'Art Contemporani

Museu d'Art Contemporàni de Barcelona (MACBA)★★
see Major Museums

Centre de Cultura Contemporània de Barcelona (CCCB)
see Major Museums

Centre d'Estudis i de Recursos Culturals *see Major Museums*

▷ *Return to La Rambla and turn right.*

Rambla dels Estudis – The second section of La Rambla was named after the first University of Barcelona, which stood here until the 19C. It is also known as **Rambla dels Ocells** (Rambla of birds), a reference to the many

Ramón Casas

The Catalan artist Ramón Casas (1866–1932) immortalized the Rambla de les Flors in several paintings. It was here, in the romantic setting of the flower stalls, that he met Júlia Peraire, who was to become his favorite model and future wife.

birds offered for sale here, along with an assortment of other creatures.

◻ *Continue to the corner of Rambla Estudis and Portaferrissa.*

Palau Moja – The clean lines and classical façade of this late 18C Baroque palace betray French architectural influences. Former home of the renowned poet **Jacint Verdaguer** (1845–1902), the building currently houses the Cultural Heritage offices of the Generalitat and also hosts temporary exhibitions.

◻ *Cross over to the corner of Rambla Estudis and C. del Carme.*

Iglesia de Betlem – The city's first public kindergartens were held in this 17/18C Baroque church, once part of a Jesuit school. Much of the sumptuous interior decoration was destroyed by fire and vandalism at the outset of the civil war in 1936, leaving only the highly ornate façade on Carrer del Carme. The interior has since been refurbished.

◻ *Continue past Iglesia de Betlem along C. del Carme to the Antic Hospital de la Santa Creu.*

Antic Hospital de la Santa Creu – The city's old hospital was founded in 1401 by King Martí I and replaced in 1929 by a new Modernist complex in L'Eixample. **La Capella**, the hospital chapel, now hosts contemporary art exhibitions (*C. Hospital 56; 93 442 71 71; open Tue–Sat noon–2pm, 4–8pm, Sun 11am–2pm*). A little way down the street, a passage leads to the long courtyard garden. Behind the carved stone façade of the former **Casa de Convalescència** (Convalescent Home) lies an entrance hall with lavish, multicolored mosaic murals and a quiet courtyard with two floors of Tuscan columns. This building now houses the head office of the Institute of Catalan Studies (*93 270 11 80; www.iec. cat*). On the left is the **College of Surgeons**. The central courtyard (the Rubio y Lluch gardens) is accessed from the rear. There's a very inviting café here.

The scale of the landscaped Gothic **Central courtyard★** is impressive. Two staircases lead to huge halls on the upper floors where hospital wards have been replaced by the books of the **National Catalan Library**, established in 1914 (*C. de l'Hospital 56; 93 270 23 00; www.bcn.es*).

Alongside this is the **Escola Massana**, the Fine Arts school.

◻ *Retrace your steps along C. del Carme to La Rambla and turn right.*

Rambla de Sant Josep – The next section of La Rambla, also known as **La Rambla de les Flors** ("flowers"), is the quintessence of the city. Flanked by plane trees brought from La Devesa Park in Girona at the end of the 19C, its flower stalls are a profusion of color and scent.

At one time this section of La Rambla was lined with monastic buildings, but anticlerical disturbances and fires put an end to this and today there are mainly sidewalk cafés, hotels, and inexpensive souvenir shops.

Palau de la Virreina★

La Rambla 99. 93 316 10 00. www.bcn.es. Open Tue–Fri 11am–2pm, 4–8pm, Sat 11am–8pm, Sun 11am–3pm.

In the late 18C, Manuel de Amat, a former Governor of Chile and Viceroy of Peru (whose main claim to fame was an affair with a Peruvian actress known as La Perricholi, later made famous as Mérimée's and then Offenbach's Périchole) returned to Barcelona with a large fortune and built this sumptuous palace, a mixture of Baroque and Rococo style. The outbuildings and landscaped courtyard in the **Centre de la Imatge** ("of the Image") provide an impressive backdrop for temporary exhibitions.

La Boqueria/Mercat de Sant Josep *see Markets*

▷ *After visiting the market, return to La Rambla and turn right.*

Rambla dels Caputxins – At the start of this section of La Rambla, also known as **La Rambla del Centre**, look out for the sidewalk mosaic designed by Joan Miró in **La Plaça de la Boqueria**, a little square located just in front of the Liceu. Note also the strange decor of the shop on the corner of the square—the **Casa Bruno Quadros** once belonged to an umbrella merchant with somewhat oriental tastes.

▷ *From Pl. de la Boqueria, take a detour along Card. Casañas to Santa Maria del Pi and Pl. de Sant Josep Oriol.*

Santa Maria del Pi★

Card. Casañas 16. 93 318 47 43. Open daily 9.30am–1pm, 5–8.30pm.

This 14C basilica was once the headquarters for some of the district's many guild fraternities.

Palau de la Virreina

©Turespaña

25

Sant Pau del Camp

©Greg Gladman/APA Publications

It stands on the pleasant little **Plaça del Pi**, which comes alive late in the day with cafés and tapas bars, and on Sundays when painters show their works. At no. 1, next to houses adorned with sgraffito, is the headquarters of the Confraternity of the Most Precious Blood, whose members accompanied the condemned to the scaffold. On the façade of the church is a large **rose window,** flanked by two unfinished towers. The **interior★** is typical of Catalan Gothic churches, with a nave and several side chapels. The lack of decoration emphasizes the architectural elements. Concerts are frequently held here.

Plaça de Sant Josep Oriol★

– Overlooked by the imposing side elevation of Santa Maria del Pi, this pretty square is home to a monument of playwright **Àngel Guimerà** (1845–1924). The square is popular with tourists, and the surrounding sidewalks are bustling with street musicians.

From Pl. de Sant Josep Oriol, continue on to C. de la Boqueria.

Turn right and return to Pl. de la Boqueria. Cross the square and follow C. de Sant Pau to the church of Sant Pau del Camp.

Sant Pau del Camp

Sant Pau 99. 93 441 00 01. Open Tue–Sat 10am–1.30pm, 4–7pm. €3.

The history of this simple church, the oldest in Barcelona, dates back to the 10C. Originally part of a Benedictine monastery, it is a fine example of Catalan Romanesque architecture, laid out on a cruciform plan. The façade is decorated with blind arches on carved supports. There are some Visigoth elements: two marble capitals with interlacing transoms on which rest the archivolt and fine reliefs of the Tetramorph and the Hand of the Almighty. Above the Baroque octagonal lantern is an openwork spire. The interior, with a single nave, is quite modest in size. The chapel of the Blessed Sacrament, the former chapter house, is accessible from the south transept.

Don't miss

* The small **cloister★** (11C–12C), with its gallery of trefoil arches, twin columns, and beautiful carved capitals, is one of the most delightful spots in the city.

Retrace your steps to Pl. de la Boqueria, exploring the streets of the Barri Xino on the way (see panel, opposite), then turn right.

Gran Teatre del Liceu★
see Nightlife

Continue along La Rambla to C. Nou de la Rambla and turn right to the Palau Güell.

Palau Güell★★ see Architects

⊳ *Retrace your steps to La Rambla. Turn left and then right into the Pg de Bacardí to Pl. Reial.*

Plaça Reial★★ – The Parisian-style iron and glass **Galería Bacardí**, off Rambla dels Caputxins, leads to this beautiful square. Lined with identical arcaded buildings (some decorated with medallions depicting sailors and explorers), it was designed in the mid-19C by Francesc D. Molina. Bars and cafés do a roaring trade here and on Sundays there is a stamp and coin market. In the center, among the palm trees, are two street lamps designed by Gaudí, an early example of his work.
One passage leads from the square to the **Carrer de Ferran**, a long shopping street full of bars, hotels, and restaurants, which connects La Rambla to Plaça de Sant Jaume. Another passage leads to the **Carrer dels Escudellers**.
Connecting these two streets, the narrow **Carrer d'Avinyó** owes its fame to Picasso, who was inspired by a visit to a brothel there to paint his seminal work *Demoiselles d'Avignon* (1907).

⊳ *Retrace your steps to La Rambla via C. Nou de Zurbano. Turn left and continue to Pl. del Teatre.*

Plaça del Teatre – This is the location of the Baroque Teatre Principal, the city's oldest theater, as well as a memorial to the poet, playwright, and founder of modern Catalan theater, **Frederic Soler** ("Serafí Pitarra," 1839–95). Caricaturists, painters, and three-card tricksters tend to favor this area.

⊳ *Continue along Rambla de Santa Mònica.*

Rambla de Santa Mònica – This is the final section of La Rambla, the point at which the avenue reaches the sea.
The **Palau Marc**, a Neoclassical building with a covered patio, is the headquarters of the Department of Culture of the Generalita, while the **Centro de Arte Santa Mònica**, housed in the former Convento de Santa Mònica, hosts temporary exhibitions (*La Rambla 7; 93 567 11 10; www.artssantamonica.cat; open Tue–Sun 11am–9pm; closed Mon except public holidays, Jan 1 & 6, Holy Saturday, May 1, Dec 25–26; no charge*).

⊳ *Next door to the Palau Marc, visit the Museu de Cera.*

Museu de Cera see For Kids

⊳ *Return to La Rambla.*

Barri Xino

Barcelona's so-called **Chinese Quarter** was traditionally a place of debauchery, vice, and red-light activity, inspiring the works of numerous writers such as Juan Marsé, Camilo José Cela, André Pieyre de Mandiargues, and Jean Genêt. However, the area has now been considerably rehabilitated and in the process has gained something of a new respectability. Its main artery, the Rambla del Raval, is lined with cafés and cultural facilities.

LA RAMBLA

BARRI GÒTIC★★

The Gothic Quarter, a maze of streets at the heart of the city, is one of Barcelona's liveliest districts. It takes its name from the 13C, 14C and 15C buildings, although it is in fact much older—ancient remains have been found here, including 4C Roman walls, still visible in places. The medieval monumental buildings were carefully restored in the 19C, giving the district its elegant appearance.

WALKING TOUR

From Plaça de Catalunya, follow the Avinguda del Portal de l'Angel to Plaça Nova, taking a detour to visit DalíBarcelona on the way.

Ⓜ *Catalunya (L1, L3).*

✗ **Lunch stop** – Cheese and wine tasting at Formatgeria La Seu, C. Dagueria 16.

DalíBarcelona *see Artists*

Plaça Nova – This square was built in 1355, when the city was being expanded. It is overlooked on one side by the Baroque façade of the **Palau del Bisbat** (Episcopal Palace) and on another by the **Collegi d'Arquitectes**, embellished with sgraffiti by Picasso. The Portal de Bisbe, flanked by two Romanesque towers, leads to the original Roman walled settlement, Barcino.

Plaça de la Seu – Linking the Plaça Nova with Via Laietana, the Avinguda de la Catedral is a large esplanade. A flight of steps leads to the Plaça de la Seu, built in 1421 at the entrance to the cathedral. The Fira de Santa Llúcia, an annual Christmas fair dating from 1786, is held here, with stands selling seasonal treats and nativity figures. The square is bordered by the Casas de la Pia Almoina, de la Canonja, and de l'Ardiaca.

▶ *Go back up the steps to Av. de la Catedral to visit the Museu Diocesà Pia Almoina.*

Museu Diocesà Pia Almoina

Av. de la Catedral 4. 93 315 22 13. www.cultura.arqbcn.cat. Open Tue–Sat 10am–2pm, 5–8pm, Sun 11am–2pm. Closed public holidays. €6.

Casa de l'Ardiaca

©Turespaña

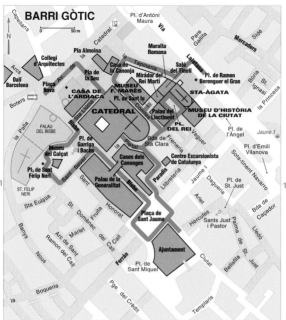

The **Pia Almoina** (1435) once housed a charitable institution, established in 1009 to provide alms for pilgrims and the poor. The adjoining **Casa de la Canonja** (1546) was a lodging for cathedral canons. Today the buildings house the Diocesan Museum, which exhibits paintings, sculptures, gold and silver, and liturgical vestments, from Romanesque to Modernist.

◗ Return to Pl. de la Seu to visit the cathedral.

Catedral Santa Eulàlia★★
see pp 30–31

◗ When you come out of the cathedral, turn into C. de Santa Llúcia to visit Casa de L'Ardiaca.

Casa de l'Ardiaca★

C. de Santa Llúcia 1. 93 318 11 95. www.bcn.es. Open Sept–Jun Mon– Fri 9am–8.45pm, Sat 9am–1pm, Jul–Aug 9am–7.30pm.

This house, built in the late 15C for Archdeacon Luis Desplà, has three façades. The main one faces the Santa Llúcia chapel, the other two face Carrer del Bisbe and Plaça de la Seu respectively. The building combines Gothic and Renaissance decorative elements. The small, peaceful **courtyard★** is a haven decorated with a frieze of glazed tiles, which, though dating from much later (1920), blends in well. The building is now home to the **Arxiu Històric de la Ciutat** (Historic City Archives).

29

Catedral Santa Eulàlia★★

Ⓜ *Catalunya (L1, L3). Pl. de la Seu.*
93 315 15 54. www.catedralbcn.org.
Cathedral: Open daily 9am–1pm,
5–7pm (choir closed on feast days
and holidays). Cloister museum:
Open daily 10am–1pm, 4–6.30pm.
Roof terrace: Open Mon–Sat
10.30am–1.30pm, 5–6pm.
Cathedral €5, Choir €2, Roof terrace
€2.20, Cloister museum €1.

Barcelona's cathedral, "La Seu"
(referring to its status as the diocesan seat), is dedicated to Saint
Eulàlia, the city's patron saint.
The first cathedral, half destroyed
during the invasion of Almanzor
(985), was replaced by another
in Romanesque style during the
11C. The present building was
started in the late 13C during the
reign of Jaume II and completed
in 1450.

The **west façade** and the spire
are recent additions (19C), built to
Gothic designs produced in 1408
by the master architect Charles
Galtès, or Carli, of Rouen, which
explains their French style.

What's inside?

♦ **Nave** The central nave and
  two side aisles were built in
  pure Catalan Gothic style. The
  slender pillars give a remarkable
  sense of height, intensified by
  subtle light from the lantern.

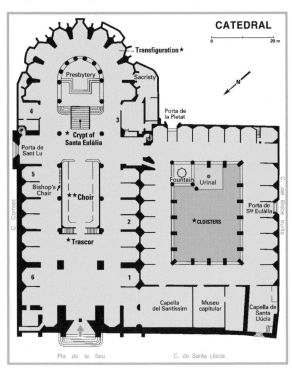

- **Capella del Santíssim**
  The 15C Chapel of the Blessed
  Sacrament, the former chapter
  house, was rebuilt in the 17C to
  house the tomb of Sant Olegar-
  ius. It houses the 15C Christ of
  Lepanto crucifix, which, according to tradition, adorned the
  prow of the galley commanded
  by Don Juan of Austria at the
  Battle of Lepanto (1571).
- **Saints' chapels** In the chapel
  dedicated to Saints Cosmas
  and Damian (1) is an impressive
  Gothic altarpiece by Bernat
  Martorell. Another chapel
  (2) contains the **tomb of
  Dominican Raimundo
  Peñafort** (14C), a much
  venerated local saint.
- **Chevet** Beneath the high altar
  is the crypt containing the
  sarcophagus of St Eulàlia★
  (14C). To the right of the presby-
  tery lie the **tombs** (3) of the
  founders of the Romanesque
  cathedral, Ramón Berenguer I
  and his wife Almodis.
- **Ambulatory chapels** These
  house Gothic and Baroque
  altarpieces, including Bernat
  Martorell's classic Catalan work,
  the **Transfiguration**★.
- **Roof terrace** Accessed via
  an elevator in an ambulatory
  chapel (4), the roof terrace
  offers magnificent **views**★★.
- **Choir**★★ The choir and nave
  are separated by an intricately
  carved Gothic screen.
  The upper choir stalls date from
  the 14C, the lower from the
  15C. The white marble **trascor**★
  (16C), begun by Bartolomé
  Ordóñez and completed
  after his death by Pierre Villar,
  has bas-reliefs depicting the
  martyrdom of Santa Eulàlia.

Choir stalls

R. Manent / Michelin

- **Chapel of the Virgin of
  Montserrat** This chapel, in the
  left-hand aisle (5), commemorates La Moreneta, the Virgin of
  Montserrat, patroness of Catalonia. Farther on, the Baroque
  retable of St Mark (6) honors
  the patron saint of shoemakers.

What's outside?
- **Cloister**★ Four galleries with
  ribbed vaults enclose the tranquil cloister, where palms and
  orange trees surround a fountain dedicated to Sant Jordi, the
  patron saint of Catalonia and
  Aragon. The gaggle of white
  geese that roam here are the
  latest in a long line of ancestors.
- **Museu capitular** The cathedral
  museum contains a number
  of 15C paintings, including
  Bartolomé Bermejo's **Pietá**, as
  well as the late medieval tomb
  of Archdeacon Luis Desplà and
  the missal of St Eulàlia, decorated with fine miniatures.
- **Capella de Santa Llúcia**
  Constructed in 1268, this is
  the only surviving part of the
  Romanesque cathedral.

Soap on the Square

The air around Plaça de Sant Felip Neri is scented with the fragrance of more than 40 types of soap emanating from the shop Sabater Hermanos, a family-run business dating back to the 1930s.

▷ *Continue along C. de Santa Llúcia, turn left into C. del Bisbe, then turn right to Pl. de Sant Felip Neri.*

Plaça de Sant Felip Neri – In this serene square is the Neoclassical church of Sant Felip Neri, built in 1752. During the Spanish Civil War, the stonework of the church's façade was pitted by executioners' bullets—the damage is still visible today, a poignant reminder of this violent period in the city's history. The building was also hit by a bomb, killing a number of children who were sheltering inside. Alongside the church is the curious **Museu del Calçat** (Shoe Museum) *(Pl. de Sant Felip Neri 5; 93 301 45 33; open Tue–Sun 11am–2pm)*, housed in the former headquarters of the Guild of Master Shoemakers.

The collection includes shoes that once belonged to famous Catalan personalities, such as the circus clown Charlie Rivel (1896–1983).

Don't miss

♦ The "shoe of Columbus"—it's the same "size" as the one worn by the famous statue of the explorer at the end of La Rambla.

▷ *From Pl. de Sant Felip Neri, return to C. del Bisbe via C. Sant Sever and turn right.*

Carrer del Bisbe – Carrer Sant Sever leads to **Plaça de Garriga i Bachs**, where the Santa Eulàlia door opens to the cathedral cloister. Opposite, on the side wall of the Baroque church of Sant Sever, is a monument by **Josep Llimona** (1864–1934), erected in memory of the inhabitants of Barcelona executed by Napoleon's troops in Ciutadella in 1809.

On the Carrer del Bisbe, between Garriga i Bachs and Plaça de Sant Jaume, lies the long façade of Palau de la Generalitat, connected by a neo-Gothic gallery (1929) to the old **Cases dels Canonges**

Neo-Gothic gallery above Carrer del Bisbe

S. Ollivier/Michelin

(Canons' Houses), a remarkable example of 14C construction.

▷ *Continue to Pl. de Sant Jaume.*

Plaça de Sant Jaume – The two main streets of the Roman city, the *cardo* (running north to south) and *decumanus* (running east to west), once passed through this square. It was at that time the *forum*, and in a way it still is, since the two buildings that symbolize the power of the city and of Catalonia —the town hall and the Palau de la Generalitat—are located here.

Palau de la Generalitat

Alan Moore/Michelin

Palau de la Generalitat

Pl. de Sant Jaume 4. 90 240 00 12. www.gencat.cat. Visit by guided tour monthly, 2nd and 4th weekend 10am–1pm, 4.30–7pm. Advance booking required. Open to the public Apr 23, Sept 11 & 24.

Before becoming the symbol of the executive of Catalonia, the **Generalitat** was a committee of the Catalan parliament consisting of two representatives from each class (clergy, aristocracy, and urban bourgeoisie), whose role was to collect taxes on behalf of the King of Aragon. The palace is a three-story building, built in the early 14C in the Gothic style, but subsequently modified. The **façade** overlooking Plaça de Sant Jaume, built in 1600 by **Pere Blay**, is a rare example of Renaissance architecture in Barcelona.

Ajuntament

Pl. de Sant Jaume 1. 93 402 70 00. Guided tours Sun and public holidays 10am–1.30pm.

The town hall was built in the last third of the 14C, but its main façade, in Neoclassical style, is later

El Call

Until the expulsion of Jews from the Iberian Peninsula in 1492, El Call (meaning "little street") was one of the largest and most prosperous Jewish communities in the Mediterranean. Behind the Palau de la Generalitat is a set of streets with names evocative of their distant past (Carrer del Call, Sant Domènech del Call, Baixada de Santa Eulàlia, Carrer dels Banys Nous)—yet, names apart, practically nothing is left of the old Jewish quarter. A significant proportion of the ghetto's population were artisans, brokers, traders, and booksellers and many owned property, not only in the Jewish quarter itself but also in the neighborhood of the community cemetery, located on Montjuïc ("mountain of the Jews"). The Museu d'Història de la Ciutat organizes guided walks around El Call.

(19C). The Gothic **side elevation** on Carrer de la Ciutat is older (c 1400) and more interesting. Its door is decorated with a stone representation of the Archangel Raphael, as well as the coats of arms of the city and the king. The original design has almost completely disappeared, as several alterations have destroyed those parts dating from the 16C and 17C. However, the **Saló de Cent★** can still be seen. This was the meeting room of the Consell de Cent, the core of the future local council. Despite the changes, its decor remains richly ornate.

▷ *Leave Pl. de Sant Jaume via C. Paradís.*

Carrer Paradís – No. 10, a Gothic building, houses the **Centre Excursionista de Catalunya**, a famous mountaineering club founded in 1876. In the courtyard are the ruins of the Temple of Augustus (see panel, opposite). Carrer Paradis opens into the Carrer de la Pietat, which runs alongside part of the apse of the

Plaça del Rei and Palau Reial Major

J. Malburet/Michelin

cathedral and is bordered on the left by the Gothic façades of the Cases dels Canonges. Facing this, the Porta de la Pietat opens into the cathedral cloister.

▷ *Turn right opposite the Cases dels Canonges onto Baixada de Santa Clara and follow this to Pl. del Rei.*

Plaça del Rei★★ – This square, which often hosts concerts and plays, is the heart and soul of the Gothic Quarter. Here we see some of the city's most important medieval buildings: the monumental ensemble or **Conjunt Monumental de la Plaça del Rei**, which includes the Royal Palace, the Capella de Santa Àgata, the Palau del Lloctinent (Lieutenant's Palace), and the Casa Clariana-Padellàs (15C). The latter, a fine example of Gothic civil architecture, which now forms part of the Museu d'Història de la Ciutat, was transferred here, stone by stone, from Carrer dels Mercaders.

Museu d'Història de la Ciutat★★ *see Major Museums*

Palau del Lloctinent – *C. dels Comtes 2. Closed to the public.* The Lieutenant's Palace (1549–57) is predominantly late Gothic in style, with Renaissance elements. It was built as the residence of the king's lieutenants—the viceroys of Catalonia—following Spanish unification. Its three façades, overlooking Plaça del Rei, Baixada de Santa Clara, and Carrer dels Comtes, are very bare. The main entrance on Carrer dels Comtes leads to a beautiful **patio**, with large arches at ground level.

Old street in the Barri Gòtic

R. Mattès/Michelin

Upstairs, there is a Tuscan gallery and an elegant staircase.

◗ *Retrace your steps and turn right along C. dels Comtes to Pl. de Sant Iu.*

Plaça de Sant Iu – This tiny square is always bustling with mime artists and musicians, which makes wandering along the street a pleasant experience. It leads to the cathedral and the Frederic Marès Museum.

Museu Frederic Marès★
see Artists

◗ *Leave Pl. de Sant Iu and continue along C. dels Comtes and C. de la Tapineria to reach Pl. de Ramón Berenguer el Gran.*

Plaça de Ramón Berenguer el Gran – Behind the statue of Ramón Berenguer III, known as the Great, by Josep Llimona, lies a small, rather plain square that opens onto Via Laietana. On the opposite side stands a large sec-tion of the 4C Roman wall that ex-tends toward Carrer de la Tapineria and Carrer de las Murallas Velles. It is 59ft/18m high. There are two floors with semicircular arched windows and three of the seven original towers are fully preserved. In the 13C, these were connected by arches to allow the construc-tion of the chapel of Santa Àgata in the **Palau Reial Major** that towers above the remains.

Temple of Augustus

At the end of Carrer Paradís, in the small courtyard of the medieval building that today houses the Centre Excursionista de Catalunya, is an unexpected sight—the ruins of a pagan temple, built in honor of Emperor Augustus. The four **Corinthian columns** (30ft/9m tall) date from the 1C BC, providing evidence of the city's Roman past. Originally, columns would have surrounded the entire building.

LA RIBERA★

In this district, which today is dedicated to art, you are at the heart of the medieval city that flourished on the shores of the Mediterranean. Here, merchants and ship owners lived in grand mansions, along with artisans, whose guilds' headquarters lay in the upper part of the district. All were united in their endeavor to build a "cathedral of the sea," a precious Catalan Gothic work of art.

🐾 WALKING TOUR

From the metro at Jaume 1, turn left along Via Laietana to Plaça Antoni Maura. From here, follow the Avinguda de Francesc Cambó to the Mercat de Santa Caterina.

Ⓜ *Jaume I (L4).*

✕ **Lunch stop** – The restaurant in the courtyard of Palau dels Marquesos de Llió (DHUB Montcada).

Mercat de Santa Caterina
see Markets

▷ *From the market, turn right then right again into C. d'En Girait El Pellisser. Turn right into C. dels Carders, then take the first left and continue on, crossing the C. de la Princesa to C. de Montcada.*

Carrer de Montcada★★ – Maritime trade has played a crucial role in the history of the city: during the 13C and 14C, Barcelona controlled Mediterranean trade, particularly to the Balearic Islands, Sardinia, Sicily, and southern Italy. Merchant families represented a stable oligarchy and ruled the city. The Carrer de Montcada, named after one of the families, was built to connect the town center to the harbor at the time, Vilanova del Mar. Along the street is a unique set of palaces, dating mostly from the late Middle Ages. In 1947, Carrer de Montcada was designated an artistic-historical heritage site.

Palau Berenguer d'Aguilar★ – *Carrer de Montcada 15.* Beyond the Carrer de la Princesa, the first street in the city to be paved, this palace

Carrer de Montcada

J. Balanya/ Michelin

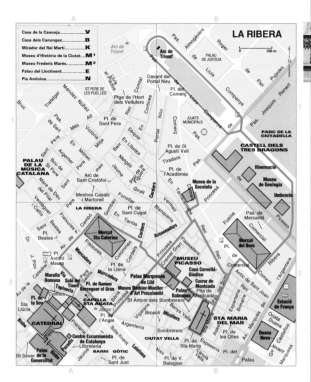

Casa de la Canonja .... **V**
Casa dels Canonges .... **B**
Mirador del Rei Martí .... **K**
Museu d'Història de la Ciutat . **M¹**
Museu Frederic Marès .... **M²**
Palau del Lloctinent .... **E**
Pia Almoina .... **P**

is the first of the medieval mansions. This magnificent residence, which was altered in the 15C and 18C, retains many architectural elements of the noble houses in medieval Barcelona, inspired by the palazzi of Italian merchants. The façade, which is very restrained, is decorated mainly around the windows on the lower floor. The wrought iron balconies are a later addition. The **central courtyard★**, which features a staircase leading to the *piano nobile*, is lightened using open arches, decorative moldings, and jars recalling the mercantile past of its owners. This palace and those alongside it, the **Palau Baró de Castellet** (No.

17), the **Palau Meca**, a Baroque building (No. 19), and the **Palau Finestres** (No. 23), house the Museu Picasso.

Museu Picasso★★ *see Artists*

Palau dels Marquesos de Lliò – *C. de Montcada 12.*
This mansion also conforms to the Catalan Gothic traditional style: a central courtyard, with stairs leading to the *piano nobile*. It owes its present appearance to alterations carried out in the 18C.
The upper façade has an open gallery, used to display items made of wool. The triple ends of the façade are a typical feature. The palace

The Montcada Family

This noble family claims to be descended from the first dukes of Bavaria. In the 12C, they acquired the viscountcies of Béarn and Bigorre when Guillem Ramón de Montcada married an illegitimate daughter of King Pedro II of Aragon. Other alliances were contracted with the royal family, the most significant being in 1322 with the marriage of Jaume II to Elisenda de Montcada, founder of the Monastery of Pedralbes (see p 56). During the Catalan conquest of Sicily, a branch of the family was established on the island. The elder branch, however, remained in Spain, where it held the highest offices.

houses **DHUB Montcada** (93 256 23 00; www.dhub-bcn.cat; open Tue–Sat 11am–7pm, Sun 11am–8pm, public holidays 11am–3pm; closed Jan 1, Jun 24, Dec 25–26; €5 (free Sun 3–8pm), an offshoot of **Design Hub Barcelona (DHUB)** (see p 81) which hosts themed exhibitions on design, graphic art, etc.

Museu Barbier-Mueller d'Art Precolombi

C. de Montcada 14. 93 310 45 16. www.barbier-mueller.ch/barce-lone. Open Tue–Fri 11am–7pm, Sat–Sun 11am–8pm, public holidays 11am–3pm. Closed Jan 1, Good Fri, May 1, Dec 25. €3.50.

Museu Barbier-Mueller

©Gregory Wrona/APA Publications

Housed in the elegant **Palau Nadal**, a 12C building restored in the 18C, this museum features a collection of pre-Columbian art, undeniably limited, but of high quality, including sculptures, gold and silver, ceramics, and fabrics representative of almost all the civilizations that existed there prior to the discovery of the Americas.

Casa Cervelló-Giudice – C. de Montcada 25. This 15C house, with patio and stairs leading to the piano nobile, was inhabited by the noble Cervelló family, then by the Giudice family, who were Genoese bankers, before being purchased by the **Maeght Gallery**.

Palau Dalmases – C. de Montcada 20. This is the mansion that retains the richest decor. A very old building, as evidenced by the late medieval-style chapel vault, it was rebuilt in the late 17C, after being purchased by the Dalmases family. The building works were closely directed by the Dalmases, who had grown rich in the textile trade. They were responsible for designing the splendid **friezes★** on the banister of the patio's covered staircase. This is decorated with fluted twisted columns

(Solomonic columns) and intertwined vines, while various mythological topics are portrayed, such as the Rape of Europa and the Chariot of Neptune.

Santa Maria del Mar★★

Pl. de Santa Maria 1. 93 310 23 90. Open Mon–Sat 9am–1.30pm, 4.30–8pm, Sun and public holidays 10.30am–1.30pm, 4.30am–8pm. No charge.

Built by Berenguer de Montagut in the 14C with unusual speed for a building of this kind (56 years), the church quickly became the spiritual center of the neighborhood. It is often colloquially called "the cathedral of La Ribera," because the port workers who lived in La Ribera financed the construction of the church, thus rivaling the bourgeois in the city who were financing the cathedral at that time. The result of that popular initiative was this wonderful church, universally praised for its symmetry and elegance.

What's inside?

◆ **Nave** The sheer beauty of this architectural marvel is immediately apparent when you enter the **interior★★★**. Santa Maria del Mar combines the two most important achievements of Catalan Gothic: purity of form and breadth of space. The architect has designed three tall naves, separated by slender octagonal pillars, achieving an effect of lightness as the interior supports are reduced to their simplest expression. The high altar is surrounded by a strange forest of columns, which join to form

©Turespaña
Santa Maria del Mar

an arch. The interior decorations have completely disappeared—the result of anticlerical disturbances in the past—but the enforced austerity serves only to highlight the architecture.

What's outside?

◆ This is one of few Catalan Gothic churches whose **exterior★★** is completely finished. Its three façades, the main one

Outside Santa Maria del Mar

The lively Plaça de Santa Maria in front of the church is a very pleasant place to stop for a break. Plaça del Fossar de les Moreres, lined with old houses with pink façades, features an eternal flame, honoring the memory of Catalan soldiers who died during the Siege of Barcelona at the end of the War of the Spanish Succession in 1714 and are buried beneath the square.

LA RIBERA

39

Below the Mercat del Born

The ruins that lie beneath the Mercat del Born are those of medieval streets, where once there stood houses, shops, and palaces. These streets survived until 1714, when Felipe V, the first Bourbon king of Spain, entered Barcelona with his French allies at the end of the War of the Spanish Succession. He ordered the demolition of the streets in order to build the Ciutadella fortress *(see **Parc de la Ciutadella★**, p 90)*, which was later itself demolished.

overlooking Plaça de Santa Maria, the second on Carrer de Santa Maria, and the third on Passeig del Born, are typical of the style: a predominance of the horizontal, with massive buttresses, many bare surfaces, and octagonal pillars.

The main façade is an object lesson in architectural expertise. Flanked on either side by statues of St Peter and St Paul, its tympanum has a large group carved on it. The 15C Flemish-style **rose window**, flanked by twin bell towers with octagonal base, is of the highest quality. The building stretches out along Carrer de Santa Maria. From this side of the church, you can take in the gargoyles, the buttresses, and the hidden stained-glass windows but, above all, the regularity of the monumental architecture. The door of the apse (which is the usual entrance) located on Passeig del Born, although in Gothic style, was built in 1542.

▶ *After visiting Santa Maria del Mar, walk all the way around the church, stopping in Plaça de Santa Maria (see panel p 39). Turn left along Pg del Born to Mercat del Born.*

Mercat del Born

©Gregory Wrona/APA Publications

MUST SEE

Museu de la Xocolata

©Gregory Wrona/APA Publications

Mercat del Born – Before moving to La Rambla in the 18C, the throbbing heart of the city was around **Passeig del Born**. Nobles followed the tournaments *(born)* that were held here, while the citizens thronged to take part in the many popular festivals.

At the end of the Passeig, where you'll find stands selling bric-a-brac and leather goods, stands the Mercat del Born, until 1973 the city's wholesale market. The work of Josep Fontseré (1874), this steel and glass structure is one of the first examples of industrial architecture in Spain. During restoration work, the remains of demolished streets were discovered beneath, which are now preserved as an archeological site. The surrounding area has been revived thanks to the popular shopping malls that have been built here.

▶ *Walk around the side of Mercat del Born and follow C. de la Ribera to the Parc de la Ciutadella.*

Parc de la Ciutadella★ *see Parks and Gardens*

Zoo Barcelona★ *see For Kids*

▶ *Follow the Pg de Lluís Companys all the way around the Arc de Triomf. Retrace your steps to the Pg del Born and turn right into C. del Rec. Cross C. de la Princesa to C. d'en Tantarantana. Take a detour to the Museu de la Xocolata in C. del Comerç.*

Museu de la Xocolata

C. del Comerç 36. 93 268 78 78. www.pastisseria.com. Open Mon, Wed–Sat and public holidays 10am–7pm, Sun 10am–3pm. €4.30.

The museum displays sculptures in chocolate made by various local confectioners, including one portraying Floquet de Neu (Snowflake), the only albino gorilla in captivity, which died in 2003 at Barcelona Zoo. There is also an interesting exhibition narrating the history of chocolate and how it captivated the palaces of Europe.

▶ *Return to C. de la Princesa, turn right and follow the road back to Via Laietana.*

LA RIBERA

L'EIXAMPLE★★

Born from Barcelona's need to expand, Eixample was a reflection of the economic boom enjoyed by the city's bourgeoisie during the 19C and early 20C, which was matched by the Renaixença, the literary movement that inspired Modernisme. You can spend a whole day exploring this fascinating area—keep looking upward as you wander around to make sure you see all the remarkably detailed façades.

✺ WALKING TOUR

From the metro at Urquinaona, start your walk with a visit to the Palau de la Música Catalana. After this, head to Plaça de Catalunya.

Ⓜ *Catalunya (L1, L3), Gracia (L3), Urquinaona (L4), Sagrada Família (L5), Lesseps (L3). The Turístic Bus stops at all the major sites. See map p 44.*

✗ **Lunch stop** – Café Zurich, Pl. Catalunya 1.

Palau de la Música Catalana★★
see Architects

Plaça de Catalunya – This huge square, comparable in size to the Place de l'Etoile in Paris, is the focal point of Barcelona for any major event, be it a key victory of Barcelona or demonstrations in support of Catalan rights. Francesc de P. Nebot built this link between the old town and Eixample (the name means

"extension") in 1927. Always lively, the square is lined with buildings of all styles. It is home to well-known businesses (the department store El Corte Ingles, Fnac…) and great cafés, ranging from the 80-year-old **Café Zurich**, which has preserved its Viennese atmosphere almost despite modernization, to the **Hard Rock Café**, where the atmosphere is naturally quite different.
This urban communications hub (Catalunya metro station is the interchange for several metro lines and trains) is decorated with sculptures by Llimona and Gargallo, and a copy of *La Deesa (The Goddess)* by Josep Clarà, a Noucentisme masterpiece. Unfortunately, the constant streams of traffic make it difficult to appreciate these works.

🔻 *Leave Pl. de Catalunya on the Rambla de Catalunya.*

Rambla de Catalunya★ –
This connects the **Gran Via de les Corts Catalanes**, the main axis of the city, with the **Avinguda Diagonal**. In this lively district, historic old-style buildings are interspersed with glass and iron structures, alongside more contemporary constructions, making for a varied and surprising mosaic.

🔻 *When you meet C. Aragó, turn right. Fundació Tàpies is on the opposite side.*

Café Zurich

J. Malburet/Michelin

MUST SEE

Lamp post of Passeig de Gràcia

P.-A. Bonneau/fotolia.com

Fundació Antoni Tàpies★★
see Artists

▶ *Continue to Pg de Gràcia.*

Passeig de Gràcia★★ – During the 19C, this road, which connected the old town to the village of Gràcia, became an upper-middle-class residential area—somewhere it was fashionable to be seen. The beautiful **lamp posts** on this broad thoroughfare are one of its defining features. Designed by Pere Falqué in 1900, they illustrate the popularity of Modernisme among industrialist clients, who were willing patrons. The *passeig* ("promenade") contains some of the most beautiful buildings in this architectural style.

▶ *Turn right on Pg de Gràcia to admire the buildings of the Illa de la Discòrdia.*

Illa de la Discòrdia★★
see Architects

▶ *Retrace your steps, cross C. Aragó, and continue along Pg de Gràcia. Take a detour along C. València to the Museu Egipci de Barcelona.*

Museu Egipci de Barcelona (Fundació Arqueològica Clos)

C. València 284. 93 488 01 88. www.museuegipci.com. Open Mon–Sat 10am–8pm, Sun 10am–2pm. Closed Jan 1, Dec 25–26. €11.

This museum has a collection representing the various periods of Egyptian civilization (plus a few pieces from the Roman period). You can pause to contemplate the sarcophagi, mummies, and funerary masks that reflect the importance of religion and life beyond the grave in the minds of Egyptians, along with collections of luxurious jewelry and household objects. A statue of Ramses II and two statues of remarkable quality from the Old Kingdom are also worth a look.

▶ *Retrace your steps to Pg de Gràcia and continue to Casa Milà.*

Passeig de Gràcia

The Catalan journalist and author Josep Pla (1897–1981) wrote of the Passeig de Gràcia: "Clearly one of its most charming features is its gentle, yet perceptible, sloping layout. The streets, sloping slightly, but just enough, make the ladies walk elegantly, lending a certain slender grace to their movements. In this sense, the Passeig de Gràcia has done a great deal for the city."

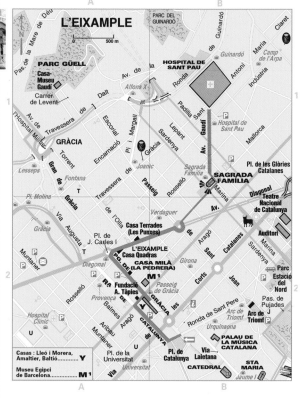

Casa Milà (La Pedrera)★★★
see Architects

▶ *Continue to Pl. de Joan Carles I and turn right along Av. Diagonal.*

Avinguda Diagonal – This long avenue runs diagonally through the city from east to west, all the way to **Pedralbes**.

Don't miss

♦ **Casa Quadras** *(No. 373, on the right-hand side of Pl. de Joan Carles I)* is a beautiful Modernist building designed by Puig i Cadafalch (1904), with Gothic

influences *(see Architects)*.

▶ *Continue along Av. Diagonal to Casa Terrades.*

Casa Terrades (Les Punxes)★
see Architects

▶ *At the next roundabout, take C. de Mallorca. At the junction with C. de la Marina, turn left for the entrance to La Sagrada Família.*

La Sagrada Família★★★
see Architects

▶ *Continue on C. de la Marina,*

The streets of Eixample

In 1863, Víctor Balaguer, the Catalan writer, historian, and politician, was tasked with selecting the names for Eixample's new streets, in his capacity as convener of the Renaixença literary movement. The first were given the names of medieval Catalan institutions: Corts, Diputació, and Consell de Cent. The next were named after areas of the kingdom of Aragon: Aragó, Valencia, Mallorca, Provença, Rosselló, and Sardenya. Finally, he honored major historical figures: Balmes, Aribau, Muntaner etc.

then bear right on Av. de Gaudí to the Hospital de Sant Pau.

Hospital de Sant Pau★
see Architects

⟩ *From here, visit Parc Güell and the Parc de la Creueta del Coll.*

Parc Güell★★ *see Architects*

Parc de la Creueta del Coll
see Parks and Gardens

⟩ *Retrace your steps to La Sagrada Família. Continue on C. de la Marina and at the junction with V. de les Corts Catalanes turn left to visit the Teatre Nacional de Catalunya (Pl. de les Arts), l'Auditori (C. Lepant), and the Agbar Tower.*

Teatre Nacional de Catalunya
see Nightlife

L'Auditori *see Nightlife*

Torre Agbar

Illuminations Apr–Oct daily 9–11pm, public holidays 9pm–midnight; Nov–Mar daily 7–9pm, public holidays 8–11pm.

Commissoned by the city's water company, this glass and steel tower is shaped like a cucumber (inspired, according to its architect **Jean Nouvel**, by the jagged mountain of Montserrat and by several of Gaudí's projects). Rising to a height of 466ft/142m—just less than the twin towers of Port Olímpic—it has a high-tech LED system that lights up its façade in constantly changing bright colors, predominantly red and blue. The tower can be seen from almost everywhere in the city and the view from the top is stunning.

⟩ *Retracing your steps from Pl. de les Glòries Catalanes, stroll down Av. Meridiana to relax in Parc Estació del Nord.*

Parc Estació del Nord *see Parks and Gardens*

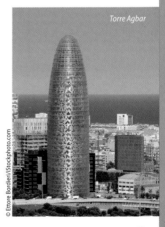

Torre Agbar

© Ettore Bordier/iStockphoto.com

L'EIXAMPLE

45

WATERFRONT★

From Montjuïc to the mouth of the Besòs, the coastline of the Catalan capital is a collection of neighborhoods with diverse atmospheres: the old port, Barceloneta, Port Olímpic, and the beaches of El Poble Nou. The rehabilitation of Barcelona's Mediterranean identity began when the city hosted the Olympic Games in 1992 and now there are plenty of pleasant places to walk—and idle away the time.

⟜⟍WALKING TOUR

The city's medieval shipyards—Drassanes—are a good place to start exploring the waterfront.

Ⓜ *Drassanes (L3), Barceloneta (L4), Ciutadella/Vila Olímpica (L4).*

✕**Lunch stop** – Escribà, Ronda Litoral Mar 42.

Drassanes★★ – The old medieval shipyards, near the Columbus monument, are the most significant to have survived from that time and provide an excellent example of Catalan Gothic civil architecture. During the reign of Pedro III "the Great" (c 1240–85), a building was erected consisting of a walled courtyard surrounded by porticos, with defensive turrets at the corners. Pedro IV "the Ceremonious" (1319–87) expanded the east and west porticos and created vaulted areas, made up of eight parallel gangways for ships, where 30 galleys could be worked on simultaneously. In the late 16C, the shipyards became the property of the Generalitat, which added eight further gangways over 330ft/ 100m in length. However, the discovery of America signaled the dominance of the Atlantic over the Mediterranean and led to the decline of the galleys. The Drassanes were dismantled and used first as

Monument a Colom

©Turespaña

MUST SEE

WATER FRONT

0 500 m

an artillery, then converted into the **Maritime Museum**.

Museu Marítim★ see Major Museums

○ After visiting the Maritime Museum, turn left and head for the Columbus Monument on Pl. del Portal de la Pau.

Monument a Colom

Pl. del Portal de la Pau. www.barcelonaturisme.com/ mirador-de-colom. Viewpoint open daily May–Oct 9am–8.30pm; Nov–Apr 10am–6.30pm. €3.

This monument, erected in memory of Christopher Columbus, towers over Plaça del Portal de la Pau, just in front of the Drassanes. Built in 1886 by Gaietà Buigas, it commemorates the return of the Genoese navigator to Barcelona, where he was received by the Catholic kings, after his first voyage to America. A large cast-iron column on a stone base bears an iron statue of the explorer. The monument has become a symbol of the identity of Barcelona, more on account of the importance attached to it by its citizens than for any particular beauty. The 170ft/52m high

Port Vell

S. Ollivier/Michelin

summit of the narrow tower (to be avoided by anyone with vertigo or claustrophobia) offers a wonderful panoramic **view**★ of the city.

⊙ *From Pl. del Portal de la Pau, take the Rambla del Mar to cross over to the Moll d'Espanya.*

Port Vell★ – The **old port** is today a very popular place of leisure. The port, which has on its left the **World Trade Center** designed by I.M. Pei, is crossed by a wooden bridge, the **Rambla del Mar**. This gives access to the Moll d'Espanya, which includes **L'Aquàrium**, the Maremagnum complex, a large shopping mall with restaurants, lively terraces, a multiplex cinema, bars and nightclubs, and the **IMAX** with its spectacular 180° screen, which offers films in 3D *(Moll d'Espanya; 93 225 11 11; www.imaxportvell.com).*

L'Aquàrium★ *see For Kids*

⊙ *Retrace your steps to Pl. del Portal de la Pau, then turn right and follow Pg de Colom to La Mercè.*

La Mercè★

Pl. de la Mercè 1. 93 315 27 56. Open daily 10am–1pm, 6–8pm. No charge.

The basilica, dedicated to the patroness of Barcelona, dates from 1760. The main façade, on the Plaça de la Mercè, is Barcelona's only example of a lightly curved Baroque façade. In Carrer Ample, the second façade, in Renaissance style, was transported here from a nearby church in 1870. The dome, an eclectic late 19C construction, is topped with a monumental statue of Mare de Deu de la Mercè (the Virgin of Mercy). The interior, with a single nave, side chapels, and a short transept, has richly decorated marble surfaces and large windows with finely wrought shutters.

Don't miss

♦ The beautiful Gothic **statue**★ representing the Mare de Deu de la Mercè by Pere Moragues (1361) is particularly interesting.

⊙ *Continue along Pg de Colom, crossing over Via Laietana to Pg d'Isabel II.*

The Consolat de Mar

From the 12C onward, merchants were the driving force that stimulated the Catalan economy. They developed trading relations with the countries of Africa and the Levant and created *alfondics*, depots that facilitated Catalan expansion in the Mediterranean. To regulate trade, in 1258 the "Consulate of the Sea" was established, a corporate body with the power to adjudicate any commercial maritime disputes. The *Libre del Consolat de Mar*, published in 1484, was the world's first treatise on maritime law and had significant influence throughout the Mediterranean. Conflicts were resolved on the basis of rules drawn up by the merchants themselves, covering all potential scenarios including the collision of vessels and losses at sea. Barcelona's Llotja (Commodity Exchange), a symbol of the power and wealth of Catalan mercantilism, was the most powerful and influential in the Mediterranean.

Via Laietana – This long straight thoroughfare, which crosses the old town from Eixample to the port, separating the Barri Gòtic and La Ribera, was opened amid much controversy in the first decade of the 20C. Houses and streets were demolished to make way for the new avenue, and many of the city guilds had to be relocated.

Continue along Pg d'Isabel II to Pl. d'Antoni López. La Llotja is on the left-hand side, with Porxos d'en Xifré opposite.

La Llotja★ – The original **Commodity Exchange** traded under a portico in the open. Goods were traded as they were landed at the port. It soon became necessary to expand these facilities and in the late 14C merchants began construction of a large building, which became the seat of the Consolat de Mar (the Consulate of the Sea). The present impressive building was rebuilt in the late 18C in Neoclassical style. The building currently serves as the headquarters of the Chamber of Trade and

Industry. All that remains of the medieval building is the great **Gothic hall★**, whose enormous proportions were matched only by the *loggia* in Florence. Its three naves, separated by triple semicircular arches, are a Mediterranean response to the narrow Gothic of northern European countries.

Porxos d'en Xifré – Following the discovery of America, many Catalans set off there to make their fortune. Many of them succeeded and subsequently returned to

©Turespaña
La Mercè

Estació de França

J. Malburet / MICHELIN

rebuilt in Neoclassical style with Rococo influences. Since 1902 it has housed the Delegació del Govern, or prefecture.

Estació de França★ – Built in 1929, France Station, a huge **iron structure** with a glass roof, is still the departure point for rail lines. It also hosts cultural events.

▷ *Retrace your steps and take the second turning onto Pl. de Palau to visit the Museu d'Història de Catalunya on Pl. de Pau Vila.*

Barcelona. These *indianos*, as they were called, frequently built magnificent private residences. One such person was **Josep Xifré i Cases** (1777–1856), who made a fortune in Cuba and became the richest man in Barcelona. All the arched Neoclassical buildings he built (including the house where the Picasso family stayed on arrival in the city in 1895) now house a whole host of crowded stores.

▷ *Continue on Av. del Marquès to Duana Nova and beyond that the Estació de França, both on the right-hand side.*

Duana Nova – This building, the New Customs House, was destroyed by fire in 1777 and

Palau de Mar – The massive silhouette of the Palau de Mar (early 20C) towers over the Moll del Dipòsit. It was originally the brick dock; carefully restored, it now houses the Museu d'Història de Catalunya.

Museu d'Història de Catalunya

Pl. de Pau Vila 3. 93 225 47 00. www.mhcat.net. Open Tue–Sat 10am–7pm (Wed 8pm, Sun and public holidays 2.30pm). Closed Jan 1 & 6, Dec 25–26. €4 (free 1st Sun of the month).

This takes you on a journey through the history of Catalonia, and there are interesting temporary exhibitions on historical themes. The building also houses the **Historical Documentation Center of Catalonia**, which holds an extensive collection of bibliographical and audiovisual materials.

▷ *Continue on to Pg de Joan de Borbó Comte de Barcelona and follow this to Torre de Sant Sebastià.*

> **Transbordador Aeri del Port**
> The Transbordador Aeri del Port *(open daily 10.45am–7pm, Jun–Sept 11am–8pm, every 15min)* runs from Torre de Sant Sebastià in Port Vell *(see p 48)* to the top of Montjuïc Mountain, passing 230ft/70m above the port. From its cabins, you get a unique **view★★** of Barceloneta and its quays.

La Barceloneta★ – This district was built in 1752 on a strip of land previously occupied by military barracks. It was designed by a military engineer, J. Martín de Cermeño, and followed a regular pattern (18 streets, of which 15 were parallel to the port). It was soon home to a population of fishermen and sailors. Despite changes in its real estate, Barceloneta has retained its popular, very Mediterranean atmosphere with its straight streets bathed in sunlight, its restaurants where the fish is the dish of choice… and, of course, its beach.

The church of **Sant Miquel del Port★** (1753), an elegant structure that dominates Plaça de la Barceloneta, is the focal point of this district, which stretches from Parc de la Ciutadella to the sea.

⊙ *Retrace your steps to Platja de Sant Sebastià and follow this to Vila Olímpica.*

Vila Olímpica★ – While Barceloneta retains some of its traditional charm, the Olympic Village is one of the city's most modern areas. Built on the coast in the industrial area of Poble Nou to accommodate the 15,000 athletes who took part in the 1992 Olympics, it has transformed Barcelona into a seaside resort.

The development project was the work of a team of eminent Barcelonans headed by **Josep Martorell**, **Oriol Bohigas**, **David Mackay**, and **Albert Puigdomènech**. Various buildings were entrusted to local architects, who received awards from FAD (Fostering Art and Design) in recognition of their contribution to the project.

©Gregory Wrona/APA Publications
La Barceloneta

Graced by beautiful gardens, dotted with contemporary sculptures, and crossed by large avenues, on fine days the Olympic Village attracts crowds who flock to the rejuvenated beaches (**Bogatell**, **Somorrostro**, **Nova Icària**), as well as the numerous cafés, bars, restaurants, and shopping malls. The **Port Olímpic Marina★★**, designed by engineer Joan Ramón de Clascá, has become one of the city's largest leisure areas.

Among the notable buildings in this area are the **two towers** (502ft/153m). The **Torre Mapfre** was designed by Iñigo Ortiz and Enrique de León, with glass façades, while the **Hotel Arts Barcelona** was designed by Bruce Graham and Frank O. Gehry. Its iron structure appears both solid and fragile. The **view★★★** from the top of these towers is truly incredible—in good weather, it is possible to see the island of Majorca on the horizon. Frank O. Gehry also designed the giant goldfish that overlooks the harbor. **Poble Nou** has become a trendy district whose studio apartments attract artists and bohemians.

MONTJUÏC

Overlooking the harbor, Montjuïc is a key part of the Barcelona landscape, with stunning views over the city. The gardens on the slopes of the hill were created in 1915 by the famous French gardener Jean-Claude Nicolas Forestier. The Universal Exhibition of 1929 saw Montjuïc's transformation, with the construction of major buildings, some of which were renovated for the Olympics in 1992.

Ⓜ Espanya (L1, L3) for the MNAC. Paral·lel (L2, L3) for the funicular to Fundació Miró. AERI cablecar from Torre de Sant Sebastià in Barceloneta for the castle and gardens.

Anella Olímpica★

Designed to host the major sporting events of the 1992 Olympics, the Olympic Ring occupies a huge plaza on the top of the hill. The Olympic Stadium and Palau Sant Jordi form the heart of this area dedicated to sport.

The **Lluís Companys Olympic Stadium★** retains its 1929 façade, but was totally refurbished internally for the 1992 Olympics *(Pg Olímpic; 93 426 20 89; open daily, except during events or concerts; May–Sept 10am–8pm, Oct–Apr 10am–6pm; no charge).*

Anella Olímpica

©Turespaña

Sports fans should visit the **Museu Olímpic i de l'Esport** (Sports Museum) dedicated to the 1992 Games and their mascot, created by the designer Javier Mariscal. *(Av. de l'Estadi 60; 93 292 53 79; www.museuolimpicbcn.cat; open Apr–Sept Tue–Sat 10am–8pm, Oct–Mar Tue–Sat 10am–6pm, Sun and public holidays 10am–2.30pm; closed Jan 1, May 1, Dec 25–26; €4).* **Palau Sant Jordi★★** is a unique indoor sports center covered by a large metal structure, designed by Arata Isozaki *(Pg Olímpic; 93 426 20 89)*, while the **Bernat Picornell pool** will appeal to those who enjoy swimming.

Other interesting constructions are the INEFC Sports Pavilion, designed by Ricardo Bofill, and a tall **telecommunications tower**, the work of Santiago Calatrava, which combines beauty and modernity.

Poble Espanyol★

Av. Marquès de Comillas 13. 93 508 63 00. www.poble-espanyol.com. Open Tue–Thu 9am–2am (Fri 4am, Sat 5am, Sun midnight), check website for holiday opening times. Shops open summer 10am–8pm (spring & fall 7pm, winter 6pm). €8.90.

This Spanish village is a reproduction of typical buildings from different regions of Spain, designed by Miquel Utrillo and

Poble Espanyol

©David Garry/iStockphoto.com

Xavier Nogues for the 1929 Exhibition. Plaza Mayor, where fairs, folk festivals, and concerts are held, is the focal point of the site. Majorcan markets, Valencian Baroque façades, Galician houses, and Castilian squares sit side by side, recreating the architectural history of Spain. The remarkable **Barrio Andaluz**, where geraniums and carnations add color to the white façades, transports you to the very heart of Andalusia. The village has more than 40 shops and artisans' workshops, making it the largest craft center in the country. Poble Espanyol has something for people of all ages—a selection of bars and restaurants, "Tablao flamenco," activities for children, and a few of the city's top nightclubs. There are also two art foundations here, Fundació Fran Daurel and Espai Guinovart. **Fundació Fran Daurel★** *(open daily 10am–7pm)* houses a collection of **contemporary art**, with some 300 paintings by major Spanish artists dating from the 1950s to the present day (Tàpies, Saura, Chillida, Picasso, Miró, Dalí, Mompó, Barceló, etc), along with a garden full of sculptures.

Don't miss
♦ **Espai Guinovart** is home to *Contorni-Entorn*, an exuberant sculpture by **Josep Guinovart** (1927–2007).

Castell de Montjuïc

Carretera de Montjuïc 66. 93 256 44 45. www.bcn.cat/castellde montjuic. Open daily Apr–Sept 9am–9pm, Oct–Mar 9am–7pm. No charge.

The first castle was built in 1640, and it was here that Catalan troops won the battle of January 26, 1714 against Felipe V. Destroyed during the War of the Spanish Succession, it was rebuilt in the 18C as a star-shaped fortress.
The castle, as the citadel, was until the mid-19C one of the strategic points of Barcelona's defensive system. It could also serve as a base to attack the city itself. Espartero took advantage of this in 1842, when he turned its guns against Barcelona, which had rebelled against the central government. For many years it also served as a military prison and it was here that the anarchist **Ferrer** was shot in 1909, and the President of the

MONTJUÏC

53

Generalitat, **Lluís Companys**, in 1940. This hated symbol of Francoist repression was transformed into a military museum, and following the closure of the latter has become an excellent place to take a walk, with exceptional views of the harbor and the city. Once it is refurbished, it is intended to host an International Peace Center, a "memorial area," and an interpretation center for the hill of Montjuïc.

Museu Etnològic

Pg de Santa Madrona 16–22. 93 424 68 07. www.museuetnologic. bcn.cat. Open Oct–May Tue, Thu, Sat 10am–7pm, Wed, Fri 10am–2pm; Jun–Sept Tue–Sat 10am–6pm, Sun and public holidays 10am–2pm, 3–8pm. Closed Jan 1, Good Fri, May 1, Jun 24, Dec 25–26. €3.50 (free Sun 3–8pm).

Built in 1973 in a very angular style, the museum is housed on three levels, of which two are used to display the collections, often as temporary exhibitions. The bulk of the collection comes from the peoples of Africa (especially Morocco) and Central America, and most of the objects, with the exception of a few representative works from pre-Columbian civilizations, belong to the modern era.

Avinguda de Miramar – This esplanade on the north of the mountain provides a beautiful panoramic **view★** of the city and, at night, of the lights of the boats sitting in its harbor. Terraces allow you to take advantage of the pleasant Mediterranean climate without being bothered by the heat. The port's AERI cable car *(93 225 27 16; open daily 10.45am–7pm with seasonal variations; €9, return €12.50)* connects the watchtower with the Torre de Sant Sebastià, located on the port side of La Barceloneta.

Plaça d'Espanya and Fira Barcelona – From the **Plaça d'Espanya**, dominated by an impressive sculpted fountain by **Miquel Blay** (1866–1936), Avinguda de la Reina Maria Cristina leads to the entrance of the exhibition park (Fira Barcelona).

Castell de Montjuïc

©Gregory Wrona/APA Publications

MUST SEE

Two **towers**, inspired by the campanile of Venice, flank the entrance. From there a beautiful **vista★** opens along the avenue, lined with Fira Barcelona flags, leading the eye to the vast **Font Màgica★**, a fountain designed by the architect and pyrotechnician Carles Buigas. At night, the jets of water are dramatically illuminated, creating the magical effect that gives the fountain its name (May–Sept Thu–Sun 9.30–11.30pm; rest of the year 7–9pm). Beyond the fountain, steps lead to the National Museum of Catalan Art.

Plaça de Sant Jordi – This square offers a magnificent **viewpoint** over the mouth of the Llobregat and the sea. At the center of the square stands a **statue of Sant Jordi★** (St George) on horseback, an imposing bronze sculpture by Josep Llimona.

Poble Sec and Paral·lel – At the foot of the hill, between Plaça d'Espanya and the sea, lies the old working-class neighborhood of **Poble Sec**, now a residential area. It is bordered by the great **Avinguda del Paral·lel**, so-called because it follows the line of latitude 41° 44' north. In the early 20C the avenue was known for its theaters and nightclubs (including the famous Molino, the Barcelona's version of the Moulin Rouge in Paris), notorious for their risqué shows—hence the area became known as the "Montmartre of Barcelona."

Fundació Joan Miró★★★ see Artists
Museu Nacional d'Art de Catalunya (MNAC)★★★ see Major Museums
Pavelló Mies van der Rohe★★ see Architects
Museu d'Arqueològia de Catalunya★ see Major Museums
Teatre Grec★ see Nightlife
CaixaForum see Architects
Jardí Botánic see Parks and Gardens
Jardins de Mossèn Costa I Llobera see Parks and Gardens
Parc de l'Espanya Industrial see Parks and Gardens
Parc Joan Miró see Artists

MONTJUÏC

PEDRALBES

The old village of Pedralbes, which takes its name from the large number of white stones *(pedres Albes)* from the mountain, is today a prestigious residential area of Barcelona with tree-lined streets and attractive architecture. The university is also located here. Its numerous parks and gardens make Pedralbes an ideal place for a walk to get away from the bustle of the city center.

Ⓜ *María Cristina (L3), Palau Reial (L3).*

Monestir Santa Maria de Pedralbes★★

Baixada del Monestir 9. 93 203 92 82. Open Apr–Sept Tue–Sat 10am–5pm; Oct–Mar Tue–Sat 10am–2pm, Sun and holidays 10am–3pm. Closed Jan 1, May 1, Good Fri, Jun 24, Dec 25. €6.

Founded in 1326 by Queen Elisenda de Montcada, a member of the illustrious family and the fourth and last wife of Jaume II, in the 14C the monastery became home to a community of Poor Clares. Plaça del Monestir lies at the entrance to the **church★**, with its spacious nave and side chapels, housing the tomb of Queen Elisenda. Only half of the interior can be visited, the other being set aside for the religious community. Outside the church, you can see the buttresses on the side elevations and the prism-shaped **spire**, which particularly impressed the French architect Le Corbusier.

Don't miss

♦ **Cloister★** This magnificent example of 14C Catalan Gothic architecture is on three levels. The bottom two, with pointed arches resting on fluted columns, enclose a beautiful courtyard with orange trees and palms. In the cloister gallery a few cells and outbuildings are open to visitors.

♦ **Sant Miquel chapel** To the right of the entrance to the Sant Miquel chapel are some very well-preserved **murals★★★** by

Murals of the Sant Miquel chapel

Palau Reial

Ferrer Bassa (1346). This artist, trained in the Italian Trecento school, manages to combine the thoroughness of the school of Siena with the scale of the Tuscan masters. The upper part is devoted to the Passion of Christ, while the delicate paintings of the Virgin in the lower section are incredibly beautiful.

Torres Trade★

The four trade towers (not to be confused with the city's World Trade Center) are a fine representation of Barcelona's architecture. They were completed in 1968 by **Josep A. Coderch**.

Palau Reial

Av. Diagonal 686.

This palace (1919–29), inspired by the Italian Renaissance palaces and surrounded by beautiful gardens, was built for King Alfonso XIII of Spain. It now houses various **fine arts and design museums**.

Gardens – Designed by the engineer Nicolau Rubió i Tudurí, the Pedralbes gardens are planted with a wide variety of bougainvillea, cypresses, pines, and cedars from around the world.

Finca Güell★ *see Architects*
Camp Nou *see Sports and Activities*
Design Hub Barcelona (DHUB)
  see Major Museums
Parc de Cervantes *see Parks and Gardens*

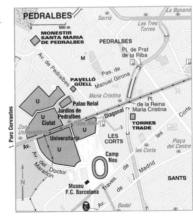

PEDRALBES

TIBIDABO

Located in the Collserola mountain range, Tibidabo overlooks Barcelona from a height of 1,745ft/532m. The mountain is dominated by a telecommunications tower, which has become a landmark for everyone in Barcelona. It is a popular Sunday walk with families who come to enjoy the park. A walk up to Tibidabo offers stunning views over the city and the sea.

T2 Tibibus from Pl. de Catalunya or train from Catalunya station to Av. del Tibidabo, then Tramvia Blau (93 298 70 00; daily except Jan 1 & 6, Dec 25–26; €4.10 return) and funicular (€4 return) or bus 111.

Collserola Tower

93 211 79 42. www.torrede collserola.com. Open Wed–Sun 11am–2pm, 3.30–6pm, 7pm, or 8pm depending on season. €5.

Below the Temple of the Sacred Heart, this communications tower was completed in 1992 by Norman Foster. A visitor platform at 377ft/115m offers panoramic views over Barcelona and its bay.

Temple del Sagrat Cor

Pl. del Tibidabo. 93 417 56 86. www.templotibidabo.info. Church: daily 8am–7pm. No charge. Viewing platform: (elevator access) open 10.30am–2pm, 3–7pm. €2.

Built around an old chapel to a design by Enric Sagnier, the Church of the Sacred Heart displays an architectural style that veers between neo-Gothic and Modernist. It was completed in 1909 and contains remarkable **frescoes**. From the old chapel (1886), an elevator takes you to a platform framed by giant sculptures of the 12 Apostles, and over this looms a huge bronze statue of Christ with outstretched arms, unveiled in 1961.

Tibidabo Amusement Park

Pl. del Tibidabo 3–4. 93 211 79 42. www.tibidabo. es. Open Jun–Aug Wed–Sun (times vary); rest of the year: weekends and holidays. Closed Jan 6– start of March. €25 (includes Sky Walk). Sky Walk: Open daily 11am–5pm. Closed Jan 1, 6, Dec 25–26). Height restrictions apply on rides.

The oldest amusement park in Spain (founded 1899) offers an extraordi-

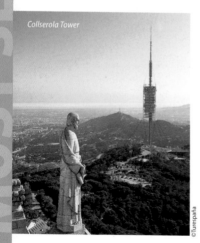

Collserola Tower

©Turespaña

Ferris wheel, Tibidabo Amusement Park

© Vatikaki/Dreamstime.com

nary **panoramic view★★** over the city, the sea, and the surrounding area. The Sky Walk guides you around the rides—these include the Talaia (1921), which takes you to a height of 1,500ft/550m above sea level, and the Avió, the world's first flight simulator (1928), as well as a ferris wheel, a carousel, and the unique and famous **Museu d'Autòmats** (Automata Museum).

CosmoCaixa, Museu de la Ciència *see For Kids*
Parc de Collserola *see Parks and Gardens*
Parc del Laberint d'Horta *see Parks and Gardens*

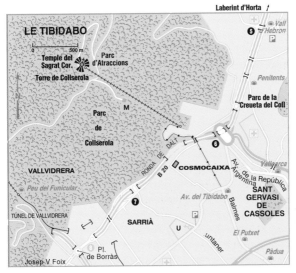

TIBIDABO

ARCHITECTS

Barcelona's architecture ranges from Roman remains to 21C towers, from medieval palaces to the extraordinary buildings that have come to define the Barcelona landscape—the works of the three main Catalan Modernista architects, Antoni Gaudí, Lluís Domènech i Montaner, and Josep Puig i Cadafalch. You will find individual examples all over the city, but all three come together in the Illa de la Discòrdia.

Illa de la Discòrdia★★

Ⓜ *Pg de Gràcia (L2, L3, L4).*
Pg de Gràcia between C. del
Consell de Cent and C. Aragó.

Illa de la Discòrdia, "the Block of Discord," takes its name from three buildings, each designed by one of these Modernist architects, as if they were competing to outshine each other on a single site. Yet the Catalan translation has lost the force of the play on words contained in the Spanish "**manzana de la discòrdia,**" alluding to the Judgment of Paris, who gave the golden apple to the most beautiful of the three goddesses, as "manzana" in Spanish means both "apple" and "block."

Casa Batlló★★ – *Pg de Gràcia 43. 93 21 603 06. www.casabatllo. es. Open daily 9am–8pm. €17.80 including audio guide.* A Gaudí masterpiece, produced at the height of his powers, this building (1904–06) has a **façade** covered with colored glass and ceramic disks, and a stunning roof covered in scales. The unique bay windows on the main floor have earned it the nicknames "House of Bones" and "House of Yawns." The interior is equally stunning. Here, Gaudí has created a work of unsurpassed beauty. Staircases, roofs, door frames and windows, the use of light—everything is directly inspired by nature. The undulation of the shapes reaches its climax with

Pavelló Mies van der Rohe

Casa Batlló and Casa Amatller

the spiral ceiling in the main hall. At the end of your visit, be sure to take in the multicolored façades of the rear terrace, with its wrought-iron balconies. Besides these emblematic buildings, the Illa de la Discòrdia includes other Modernist residences, such as **Casa Ramón Mulleras** (1911) by Enric Sagnier, and Jaume Brossà's **Casa Bonet**.

Casa Amatller★ – *Pg de Gràcia 41. 93 48 772 17.* This building by Puig i Cadafalch (1900) has a beautiful façade with floral fres-coes. The large Gothic windows, a favorite device of the architect, and the railings of balconies and gates are superbly delicate. Today the building houses the Fundació Institut Amatller d'art Hispanic.

Casa Lleó i Morera★ – *On the corner of C. del Consell de Cent.* This large stone building (1905) is the work of Domènech i Montaner. The plant-themed decor focuses on the balustrades and around the bay windows. Look up to see the decorative crest and niche that top the building.

Pavelló Mies van der Rohe★★

Ⓜ *Espanya (L1, L3). Av. Francesc Ferrer i Guàrdia 7. 93 423 40 16. www.miesbcn.com. Open daily 10am–8pm. €4.50.*

This pavilion was designed by Mies van der Rohe for the 1929 International Exhibition and was considered a model of rationalist architecture. The original was dis-mantled after the exhibition, and the building seen today is an exact copy (1986). The pavilion houses the headquarters of the Mies van der Rohe Foundation.

ARCHITECTS

GAUDÍ

Antoni Gaudí was born in Riudoms, southern Catalonia, in 1852. After studying architecture at Barcelona's Escuela Técnica Superior de Arquitectura, he went on to develop the strikingly unique style that plays such a huge role in the modern cityscape. His inspiration is said to have come from the long walks in nature he took as a child, coupled with a fierce sense of Catalan pride and a profound spirituality. Critics of this eccentric character are never quite certain whether he was an absolute genius—or quite simply insane. Gaudí died in 1926 and is buried in the crypt of his beloved (and still unfinished) Sagrada Família.

Casa Milà (La Pedrera)★★★

Ⓜ *Diagonal (L3, L5). Pg de Gràcia 92. 90 240 09 73. www.fundacio caixacatalunya.org. Open daily Mar–Oct 9am–8pm; Nov–Feb 9am–6.30pm. Closed Jan1 & 6 and 2nd week, Dec 25–26. €11.*

Commonly known as La Pedrera ("the quarry"), this building was

Works of Antoni Gaudí
In 1985, Parc Güell, Palau Güell, and Casa Milà were designated UNESCO World Heritage Sites. The Nativity façade and crypt of Sagrada Família, Casa Batlló, Casa Vicens, and the crypt of Colònia Güell were added in 2005 to create the site collectively known as the "Works of Antoní Gaudí."

designed for the wealthy Milà family. It is quite simply an explosion of fantasy. The **façade★★** displays an architecture full of subtleties reminiscent of the movement of the sea. Be sure to look at the bars on the windows and the wrought-iron balcony railings.

Attic and roof terrace★ – *Elevator access.* The parabolic arches in the attic define a discrete space, which hosts the **Espai Gaudí**, where studies, models, photographs, and films recount the life and work of the architect. After the attic, a flight of stairs provides access to an unexpected roof terrace, where you can take a trip

Roof terrace of Casa Milà

©Turespaña

through a magical forest of whimsical forms and curved shapes, populated by disturbing ceramic "warriors." The **views★** of Barcelona from here, including the Sagrada Família, are quite spectacular.
El Pis★ – Upstairs, the **apartment** consists of two sections: the reconstruction of the inside of a bourgeois home of the early 20C and an exhibition on Barcelona at that period. Here, you will find the furnishings (all curved), electrical appliances, and daily accoutrements of a wealthy family.
Once you have come back down, remember to take a look up from the atrium—the sinewy and phantasmagoric shapes will make you dizzy. The mezzanine floor houses temporary exhibitions.

Other Gaudí houses include:

Finca Güell (Pedralbes)★ – *Av. Pedralbes 7*. Here, Gaudí designed the gatehouse, stables, and gate for Eusebi Güell's country estate. The wrought-iron gate features an extraordinary reptile poised to attack, known locally as the Drac ("dragon") of Pedralbes.

Bellesguard's Tower (Casa Figueras) – *C. de Bellesguard 16–20*. The fanciful appearance of this house near the Collserola mountain (1900–1909) was inspired by the remains of the medieval castle that once occupied the site.

Casa Calvet – *C. de Casp 48*. Built for a textiles manufacturer in 1898–1900, this is deemed to be the most conventional of Gaudí's designs. However, it is not without its witty elements—for example, the columns on either side of the

©Greg Gladman/APA Publications

Bar Marsella
This authentically shabby little bar in Carrer de Sant Pau, opened in 1820, is reputed to have been a regular haunt of Gaudí, as well as some of Barcelona's other great artistic minds such as Dalí and Picasso. The house specialty is absinthe, a highly contentious liquor that was banned in many countries (although not in Spain) for almost a hundred years.

entrance are in the form of stacked bobbins, a nod to the success of the family business that funded the project.

Casa Vicens – *C. de les Carolines 24*. This house (1883–88), which displays a marked Moorish influence, was the first significant project of Gaudí's career. It was commissioned by Manuel Vicens, the wealthy owner of a ceramics factory—hence the green and white checkered ceramic decoration, with floral details, that adorns the façade.

ARCHITECTS

La Sagrada Família

J. Malburet / Michelin

Josep M. Bocabella, the founder of a fraternity dedicated to St Joseph, wanted to establish its main seat in a church inspired by the Sacré-Cœur in Paris. Construction began in 1882 to a design by Francesc del Villar, but quickly came to a halt when the architect resigned. The following year Gaudí was appointed to the project, which he completely transformed, and to which he was to devote the rest of his life. The symbolism he portrayed became more complex every day, to the point of complete obscurity.

At the time of Gaudí's death, only the crypt, the apse, and the Nativity façade had been completed. Since then the work has continued, more or less rapidly, financed by donations, and it is estimated that the sanctuary could be completed around 2030.

Josep Maria Subirachs (b. 1927) has produced angular sculptures for the Passion façade. Gaudí would no doubt have appreciated the symbolism of the "magic square" on this façade, with a constant of 33—the age of Christ at the time of the Passion.

⛪ La Sagrada Família★★★

Ⓜ *Sagrada Família (L2, L5). 93 207 30 31. www.sagradafamilia.cat. Open daily Apr–Sept 9am–8pm; Oct–Mar 9am–6pm (Jan 1 & 6, Dec 25–26 2pm). €12.*

Dedicated to the Holy Family and St Joseph, this is Gaudí's most well-known work. It is Spain's most visited monument, and among the most visited in Europe—you only have to witness the queues forming outside at 8 o'clock in the morning to appreciate this.
For its creator, who was once described as "God's architect," it was a symbol of atonement for the materialism of the modern world and an expression of brotherhood among peoples.

What's inside?

♦ **Nave** A visit to the interior is accompanied by the din of construction equipment, but this does not detract from the

Gaudí's vision of his masterpiece

Constructed in the form of a Latin cross, La Sagrada Família was intended to have three façades, dedicated to Christ's Nativity, Passion and Death, and Glory. Each was to be flanked by four towers symbolizing the 12 Apostles. On the apse, a large tower was to be dedicated to the Virgin, while the spire of the transept, symbolizing Christ, would be surrounded by four towers dedicated to the Evangelists.

MUST SEE

fascination of the monument. As it currently stands, you will catch a startling glimpse of the impressive forest of columns in the nave designed by Gaudí. The columns, dedicated to Christian cities and continents, represent the apostles. There are also some stained-glass windows, including the rose window by Joan Vila-Grau (2001). The four towers on each of the two façades *(access by elevator; closed in adverse weather; €2.50)* offer remarkable **panoramic views★★**.

◆ **Crypt** Gaudí is buried in the crypt, now converted into a fascinating museum-workshop, which outlines plans, models, drawings, and projects, as well as photos showing the progress of the work at various periods.

What's outside?

◆ **Nativity façade★★** Four towers rise to a height of 377ft/ 115m above the three portals of the façade. On the left is the portal of Hope; in the center, the portal of Charity, decorated with a vast array of floral motifs above the genealogy of Jesus;

Gaudí's death

Gaudí's life came to a tragic and somewhat extraordinary end. On June 7, 1926 he was run over by a tram at the intersection of Carrer de Bailén and the Gran Vía. He was shabbily dressed, as was his wont, and in spite of his fame and popularity in Barcelona (half the city took to wearing black upon hearing the news of his death), he was taken for a vagrant and hauled off to the Antic Hospital de la Santa Creu—a pauper's hospital. When his friends discovered him, they wanted to move him, but Gaudí was adamant: "I belong here among the poor." He died a few days later, on June 10, aged 74.

and on the right, the portal of Faith, decorated with sculptures illustrating the childhood of Jesus and the Visitation.

The Sagrada Família is scheduled to be consecrated by Pope Benedict XVI on November 7, 2010.

©Alex Nikada/iStockphoto.com

Interior of La Sagrada Família

ARCHITECTS

65

"Spire" of Palau Güell

©Archives/iStockphoto.com

Palau Güell★★

Ⓜ Liceu (L3). C. Nou de la Rambla 3–5. 93 317 39 74. www.palauguell. cat. Currently closed for restoration.

This spectacular residence, built by Gaudí between 1886 and 1890, is indeed a work of his early years, reflecting his own very idiosyncratic idea of architecture, and his desire to go beyond the historicist style so prevalent at that time. On the white stone **façade★** can be found Catalan symbols such as the dragon and the "four bars" from the Catalan flag, along with imaginary motifs and the initials of **Eusebi Güell**. It has two enormous parabolic arches

at the entrance, and a beautiful wrought-iron gate, flanked by two serpents. The innovative use of materials, the treatment of light, used as a method of integrating the different areas, and the use of wood for the coffered ceilings of the rooms are some of the key features to look out for when visiting this magnificent mansion.

Highlight

◆ **The Grand Hall** The palace's most impressive room, the central Grand Hall occupies three floors. Its magnificent parabolic cupola is full of eyelets that allow light to filter through, reminiscent of the night sky

As with his other buildings, Gaudí gives free rein to his imagination on the terrace: the undulating floors and dreamlike chimneys around the huge lantern in the Grand Hall are lined with mosaics.

Parc Güell★★

Ⓜ Lesseps (L3), then follow signs. Take Bus 92 from Hospital de Sant Pau. Olot 1. 93 413 24 00. www.bcn.cat/parcsijardins. Open daily 10am–6pm (on fine days 9pm). No charge.

Undulating seat at Parc Güell

S. Ollivier /Michelin

Church of Colònia Güell

The best known of the commissions entrusted to Gaudí by Güell, this was intended to be the main garden of the city but was never completed. The park opens onto two fairy-tale buildings shaped like toadstools. Stairs guarded by a dragon lead to the **Hall of the Hundred Columns**. This grand space, which was intended to be used as a market and which in fact has only 86 slanting Doric columns, is magnificent. The mosaic on the undulating roof is covered in ceramic shards, the famous *trencadís*. Above this seemingly endless **undulating layer★★**, which lies in turn above the hall of columns, there is a large circular room, which offers a tremendous **vantage point** over the city.

Don't miss

♦ **Casa-Museu Gaudí★** 93 219 38 11. www.casamuseugaudi.org. Open daily Apr–Sept 10am–8pm (Oct–Mar 6pm). Closed Jan 1 & 6, Dec 25–26. €5.50. To round off your tour of this magical place, go inside the house where the architect lived from 1906 to 1926. Here you will discover a collection of furniture designed by Gaudí.

Church of Colònia Güell

Train from Pl. Espanya to Colònia Güell station. 93 630 58 07. www.elbaixllobregat.net/coloniaguell. Open May–Oct Mon–Fri 10am–2pm, 3–7pm, public holidays 10am–3pm except during mass (Sun, public holidays 11am, 1pm, 8pm). €4.

Construction of the church at Colònia Güell *(see p 97)* began in 1908, to a design involving two aisles and a central tower (130ft/40m). Even though Eusebi Güell abandoned the project in 1914, when only the lower nave was completed, Gaudí had still had time to test numerous architectural innovations, which he then used in the construction of the Sagrada Família. Note the perfect use of forms and materials so typical of the architect, including the two huge shells acting as a font and the brick roof illuminated by multicolored floral stained-glass designs. Note too the design of the church's confessional.

ARCHITECTS

LLUÍS DOMÈNECH I MONTANER

Lluís Domènech i Montaner, who was born in Barcelona on December 21, 1850, is considered alongside Gaudí to be one of the most important and innovative architects of the Modernist era. He was registered as an architect in the city by the age of 23 and went on to become a professor and director at the Escuela Técnica Superior de Arquitectura. Like Gaudí, Domènech was an avid patriot and played a significant role in Catalonia's quest for autonomy. Domènech died on December 27, 1923, just a few days after his 74th birthday, leaving a legacy of striking architectural treasures.

Castell dels Tres Dragons★★

Ⓜ *Arc de Triomf (L1). Pg de Picasso entrance to the Parc de la Ciutadella.*

Domènech constructed this monumental Gothic building, in exposed red brick with iron supports, in 1887. Located in the Parc de la Ciutadella *(see p 90)*, its purpose was to house the café-restaurant for the 1888 Universal Exhibition. It is now home to the Zoology Museum. The crenellated walls, the large, Gothic-inspired windows, and the Romanesque turrets at each corner lend the castle a medieval fairy-tale feel. The ceramic crests around the top of the building, designed by Alexandre de Riquer and Joan Llimona, are painted with allegorical figures and fantastic images. The interior is light and airy but relatively unadorned.

The building takes its name from a comedy written in 1865 by the Catalan playwright Serafí Pitarra.

Palau de la Música Catalana★★

Ⓜ *Urquinaona (L1, L4). Sant Francesc de Paula 2. 90 244 28 82. www.palaumusica.org. Open 9.30am–3.30pm (Easter week and Aug 6pm). €12. Guided tours available.*

Castell dels Tres Dragons

© Turespaña

Palau de la Música Catalana

©Turespaña

In the narrow Carrer de Sant Pere més Alt, this unique monument, a Modernist masterpiece, is the most prominent symbol of the Catalan identity from the early 20C. It was built by Lluís Domènech i Montaner between 1905 and 1908 on behalf of the **Orfeó Català**, a choral society founded in 1891 by Lluís Millet (1867–1914) in order to promote Catalan popular music. In 1909 Barcelona City Council presented Domènech with a "best building" award in recognition of his creation.

The building was enlarged and completely transformed in 1989, while the recent renovation of the neighborhood allows a fuller view of its spectacular **exterior★**. The colorful mosaics and sculptured group in the upper corner of the main entrance, representing popular song, were created by Miquel Blay.

The concert hall is breathtaking. To the left of the stage, a bust of **Josep Anselm Clavé** (1824–74), the founder of numerous popular choirs, symbolizes Catalan music. To the right of the stage stands the extraordinary **Ride of the Valkyries**, flanked by a bust of Beethoven. This dynamic sculpture by Gargallo represents international music, complementing the mosaic silhouettes and the bust in relief that Eusebi Arnau placed at the back of the stage. The place is filled with a host of surprising touches; it is somewhere that you really must visit.

Don't miss

♦ Look up to view the magnificent **inverted dome★★**. Made of polychrome glass, it throws a gentle light and lends a delicate touch to the interior.

World Heritage Site

The Palau de la Música Catalana and the Hospital de Sant Pau were added to UNESCO's list of World Heritage Sites in 1997. The buildings are effusively described as "masterpieces of the imaginative and exuberant Art Nouveau that flowered in early 20th-century Barcelona."

ARCHITECTS

69

Hospital de Sant Pau

©Turespaña

Domènech collaborated with the sculptors **Pablo Gargallo** and **Eusebi Arnau** over the ornamentation of the complex. The pavilions that housed the wards are adorned with glazed ceramic tiles depicting mythological and historical themes, which were intended to cheer the patients and speed their recovery.

A fully functioning hospital until 2009, the building no longer houses any hospital departments and is currently being restored for use as a museum and cultural center.

Hospital de Sant Pau★

🅼 *Sant Pau (L5). Av. Sant Antoni María Claret 167. 93 317 76 52. www.santpau.es. Visit by guided tour only 10am, 11am, noon, 1pm. Closed Jan 1 & 6, Dec 25–26. €6. Access to the grounds is free.*

Located on a large site at the end of the broad Avinguda de Gaudí, the beautiful red-brick Hospital de la Santa Creu i de Sant Pau was designed by Domènech and built between 1901 and 1930 to replace the medieval complex now referred to as the "Antic" hospital *(see p 24)*. The new complex is considered to be the most significant building in Catalan Modernisme, and won the architect his third "best building" award (the second was for Casa Lléo, *see p 60*).

The wings of the main building are curved to represent Charity, a reflection of the original hospital foundation whose mission was to offer aid to pilgrims and the poor. The wards were housed in a number of pavilions, which were linked to the central facilities via underground corridors.

Casa Fuster

🅼 *Diagonal (L3, L5). Pg de Gracia 132.*

Located on the corner of Carrer Gran de Gracia, Casa Fuster was built in 1908–11 as a gift from one Mariano Fuster to his wife. The building's relatively flat façade is considered to reflect Domènech's transition to a more restrained style of ornamentation. In the 1920s the house changed hands and became a cultural hub. The building narrowly escaped demolition in the 1960s—the result of loud protest from the entire city—and was instead restored. Today it houses a luxury hotel.

Don't miss

♦ The **Café Vienés** opened in the 1920s on the ground floor, attracting the city's artists and intelligentsia. Substantial columns with decorated capitals support the vaulted ceiling, reminiscent of ecclesiastical architecture—although there the resemblance ends!

Casa Lamadrid

🅜 *Girona (L4). C. Girona 113.*

Casa Lamadrid is a tall, narrow, symmetrical building constructed in 1902. The decorative stone balconies at first-floor level, elegant wrought-iron balconies with stone floors on the upper façade, and carved ornamentation on top of the building set it apart from its more austere neighbors.

Casa Thomas

🅜 *Girona (L4). C. Mallorca 293.*

Built in 1898 for Josep Thomas, a printer, Casa Thomas is a neo-Gothic fantasy, with a row of three arched windows flanked by a pair of oriel windows set into square turrets. Domènech's original design was for a two-story building, with the printworks at ground level and the family's living accommodation above. His son-in-law, Francesc Guàrdia, was responsible for adding the upper levels.

Editorial Montaner i Simón

🅜 *Pg de Gracia. C. Aragó 255.*

This building (1879–85), Domènech's first major project in the city, was constructed in brick, iron, and glass to house a publishing company. The literary theme is reflected in the ornamentation on the façade, which includes busts of great writers. Natural light floods into the interior through a large skylight, and the neat rows of slender columns lend a graceful but distinctly industrial feel. Since 1989, the building has formed an elegant backdrop to a collection of works by Antoni Tàpies *(see p 88)*.

Don't miss

♦ The eye-catching jumble of aluminum cable that tops the building is Tàpies' sculpture *Núvol i Cadira (Cloud and Chair)*.

Palau Ramon de Montaner

🅜 *Diagonal (L3, L5). C. Mallorca 278.*

Palau Montaner, completed in 1893, is an ornate Italianate mansion that today looks curiously squat beside the tall modern buildings that surround it. It was designed for one of the owners of the publishing company Editorial Montaner i Simón *(see previous entry)*. The project was initially begun by Josep Domènech i Estapà but completed by Domènech i Montaner, assisted by the sculptor Eusebi Arnau and the stained-glass artist Antoni Rigalt. It now houses the Spanish government in Barcelona.

Casa Fuster

Alan Moore/Michelin

JOSEP PUIG I CADAFALCH

Born in Mataró in 1867, Cadafalch qualified as an architect in Barcelona and Madrid. A follower of Lluís Domènech i Montaner, he is considered to be one of the last representatives of Modernisme and one of the first of the subsequent Noucentisme. Cadafalch was also involved in politics and from 1917–23 was president of the Mancomunitat ("Commonwealth") de Catalunya, although he fell foul of the coup by the Spanish dictator Primo de Rivera and was sacked as architect for the 1929 Universal Exhibition. From 1942 until his death, he was president of the Institut d'Estudis Catalan. When Cadafalch died in Barcelona in 1956 at the age of 89, he too left an impressive list of buildings in and around the city—those described below are just a sample.

Casa Terrades (Casa de les Punxes)★

Ⓜ *Verdaguer (L4, L5). Av. Diagonal 416, at the junction with C. Rosselló and C. Bruc. Closed to the public.*

Casa Terrades

©Turespaña

Les Quatre Columnes

An interesting story is attached to the Four Columns that Cadafalch created in Montjuïc, where the **Font Màgica**★ now stands *(see p 55)*. The columns, erected in 1919, represented the four red stripes of the Catalan flag. However, their symbolism offended the dictator Primo de Rivera, and the columns were demolished in 1928, the year before the Universal Exhibition, thus guaranteeing that they would not draw attention to the Catalan quest for autonomy.

This extraordinary but magnificent triangular neo-Gothic castle (1905), which stands somewhat incongruously on the Avinguda Diagonal, is known as the Casa de les Punxes (House of Needles) because of the spikes that top the pointed roofs. The building surrounds a core of three houses that already occupied the site. These were originally owned by three sisters of the Terrades family, who commissioned Cadafalch to link them into one behind a new façade. The wrought-iron balconies were designed by Manuel Ballarín, the sculptural reliefs by Alfons Joyol, and the stained-glass windows by Eduar Amigó.

CaixaForum

Ⓜ *Espanya (L1, L3). Marqués de Comillas 6–8 (corner of C. de Mèxic).*

Located in Montjuïc, this beautiful building was designed for Casimir Casaramona i Puigcercós as a

MUST SEE

Casa Martí

textile factory. Bare brickwork is topped by Catalan vaults resting on cast-iron columns, with battlements and towers completing the medieval effect. Construction was completed in 1911 and the factory immediately received the City Council award for the best industrial building—deservedly so, as the charming neo-Gothic exterior and well-lit, spacious interior are a far cry from the conventional idea of a factory. The textile operation was closed down only seven years later and the building was used first as a warehouse and then as premises to house the transport, both equine and motor, of the National Police Force. "La Caixa" purchased the building in 1963; in the 1990s it was refurbished and transformed into a cultural center for the city *(see p 80)*. The striking entrance was redesigned by the Japanese architect **Arata Isozaki**.

Casa Martí (Els Quatre Gats)

Ⓜ *Catalunya (L1, L3), Urquinaona (L4). C. Montsió 3. Open daily 10am–2pm.*

A gem of a building tucked away in a side street in the Barri Gòtic, Casa Martí was constructed by Cadafalch in 1896.

The exterior is a delightful neo-Gothic façade, with wrought-iron balconies, stained glass, and sculptures by Eusebi Arnau, including a substantial figure of Sant Jordi. Look out for the poster designed by Picasso! The ground floor is occupied by **Els Quatre Gats**, a café-restaurant on the site of the original, which, around the turn of the 20C, was a meeting place for the city's intellectuals and bohemians. Picasso held his first exhibition here *(see p 82)*.

In pursuit of Modernisme

A great way to take in the works of Barcelona's Modernista architects is to follow the Modernisme Route. This guides you around 115 examples of their work, ranging from the attention-grabbing Sagrada Família to the less obvious benches and lamp posts that you might so easily miss *(www.rutadelmodernisme.com)*.

ARCHITECTS

MAJOR MUSEUMS

Barcelona has a satisfyingly diverse list of museums to visit, from the magnificent Museu Nacional d'Art de Catalunya to the collections of decorative arts, textiles, and ceramics housed in the Palau de Pedralbes. Visits to the museums included in this section will acquaint you with the essence of Barcelona and of Catalonia and you will soon understand what lies behind the Catalans' pride in their identity.

Museu Nacional d'Art de Catalunya (MNAC)★★★

🚇 *Pl. Espanya (L3, L6). Palau Nacional, Parc de Montjuïc. 93 622 03 76. www.mnac.cat. Open Tue–Sat 10am–7pm, Sun and public holidays 10am–2.30pm. Closed Jan 1, May 1, Dec 25. €8.50 (free 1st Sun of the month).*

The National Museum of Catalan Art is housed in the stately Palau Nacional in Montjuïc, built for the 1929 Universal Exhibition and famous for its **Oval Hall**. The collection is divided into five sections.

Romanesque Art★★★ – Rooms 1–8. A visit here is an absolute must! The collection is extraordinary, especially as regards mural paintings, and is superbly presented. The frescoes, transferred here from their churches of origin between 1919 and 1923 to prevent their unauthorized export, are presented in "chapels" and large rooms recreating the layout of the churches of the time. Highlights include:

- ◆ The paintings (12C) from the church of Sant Joan de Boi.
- ◆ The lateral apses of Sant Quirce de Pedret (1090–1120).
- ◆ The beautiful Epiphany from the 12C Santa Maria de Taüll.
- ◆ The extraordinary **Pantocrator** (c 1123) from Sant Climent de Taüll, one of the masterpieces of Romanesque painting.
- ◆ The paintings from the church of San Pedro de Arlanza (1210), near Burgos.
- ◆ The **Majestat Batlló**, a mid-12C polychrome crucifix on display in the sculpture rooms.

There is also a magnificent **collection★** of capitals, gold and silverwork, and enamels. The section concludes with paintings from the Chapter House of **Sigena** (1200).

Museu Nacional d'Art de Catalunya

©Turespaña

MUST SEE

Gothic Art★★ – *Rooms 9–17*.

This journey through the world of Catalan Gothic art (13C–15C) includes Barcelona's most important painters (Guerau Gener, Joan Mates, Ramón de Mur, Joan Antigó, Bernardo Despuig, and Jaume Cirera), along with a large international Gothic collection. Highlights include:

Conquest of Majorca by Jaume I *in the Gothic Art collection*

R. Manent/Michelin

+ The **Bernat Martorell** room.
+ The *Virgin of the Councillors* by **Lluís Dalmau** (1443–45).
+ The *Consecration of St Augustine* (c 1466–75) by **Jaume Huguet**.
+ The works of the **Master of La Seu d'Urgell**.
+ The room devoted to 14C and 15C funerary sculpture.
+ The stone altarpiece attributed to **Jaume Cascalls**.

Renaissance and Baroque Art – *Rooms 18–22 (Renaissance), 23–25 (Baroque)*.

Major artists in this collection of 16–18C works include Spaniards Ayne Bru, Pere Nunyes, Pedro Berruguete, Francisco de Zurbarán, José de Ribera, Velázquez, and El Greco. Italian artists include Fra Angelico, Tintoretto, and Annibale Carracci. There are also portraits by Quentin de la Tour and works by Rubens, Cranach the Elder, and Fragonard. Highlights include:

+ Fra Angelico's **The Madonna of Humility★**(c 1443).
+ *The Immaculate Conception* by Francisco de Zurbarán (1632).
+ José de Ribera's *The Martyrdom of St Bartholomew* (1634).
+ Velázquez' *St Paul* (1619).
+ Rubens'The *Virgin and Child with St Elizabeth and the Infant St John the Baptist* (1615).

Modern Art – *Rooms 26–35*.

This collection demonstrates the explosion of artistic creativity that took place in Barcelona between the 19C and the Spanish Civil War. All the movements (Academism, Surrealism, Modernisme, Noucentisme, Impressionism, etc) and big names are represented—Mariano Fortuny, Pablo Picasso, Ramón Casas, Santiago Rusiñol, Isidre Nonell, Joaquim Mir, Joaquim Sunyer, and Salvador Dalí. There are also works by the sculptors Josep Llimona, Pablo Gargallo, and Julio González.

Highlights include:

+ Picasso's *Woman in a Hat* (1937).
+ *Casas and Pere Romeu on a Tandem* by Ramón Casas (1897).
+ Dalí's unusual *Portrait of the Artist's Father* (1925).
+ Isidre Nonell's *La Paloma* (1904).
+ Furniture designed by Gaudí, in the Modernisme collection.

Drawings, prints, and posters – Selected works include Fortuny's Modernist collection.

Numismatics – This rich collection of coinage that has been in circulation in Catalonia includes items issued by the Greek colonies at Empúries and Roses, and even modern credit cards.

Museu d'Art Contemporàni de Barcelona (MACBA)★★

Ⓜ Catalunya (L1, L3).
Pl. dels Àngels 1. 93 412 08 10.
www.macba.es. Open Jul–Sept
Mon & Wed 10am–8pm, Thu & Fri
11am–midnight; Oct–Jun Mon
& Wed–Fri 11am–7.30pm; year-
round Sat 10am–8pm, Sun and
public holidays 10am–3pm.
Closed Jan 1, Dec 25. €7.50.

Built by American architect Richard
Meier, the **building★★** is inspired
by the Mediterranean rationalist
tradition, emphasizing natural
light. In front of the museum's
white frontage is a pleasant courtyard, accessed from La Rambla via
Carrer de Bonsuccés, one of the
neighborhood's most attractive
streets, and Carrer Elisabets. Here,
in contrast with the geometric
lines of the museum, the old
Gothic church of the Convent
dels Àngels, now restored, houses
a temporary exhibition space
dubbed the "**capella MACBA.**"
The museum's vast white rooms
are the perfect setting for the **permanent collection★**, comprising
some 1,500 works from the second
half of the 20C, where special em-
phasis is placed on Catalan contri-
butions and on foreign trends that
have had a particular influence on
contemporary Catalan art.
The collection includes representative constructivist and abstract
works—*Beschwingt Bindungen* by
Paul Klee, two mobiles by Alexander Calder, the *Concetto Spaziale*
by Lucio Fontana, *Woman in the
Night* by Joan Miró, *Planos de color
con dos maderas superpuestas* by
Joaquín Torres-García, and beautiful variations on the *Desocupación
No cubica del espacio* by Jorge
Oteiza—as well as more experimental work, such as *Réserve des
Suisses morts* by Christian Boltanski,
Das Glab in den Lüften by Anselm
Kiefer, and *Portrait* by Muntadas.

Museu d'Art Contemporàni de Barcelona

MUST SEE

There are also representative pieces from the 1980s—Joan Hernández Pijuan's *Tríptic Granada*, *Dues creus negres* by Antoni Tàpies, Alberto Refols Casamada's *Pintura 2* (a homage to Joan Miró), and José María Sicilia's *Black Flower*.

Don't miss

- The painting *Season of Rain No. 2* (1990), the work of the Mallorcan Miquel Barceló, is a personal interpretation of the rain as a symbol of fertility and regeneration.
- *Asociación Balnearia 2* (1987), a sculpture by Susana Solano, in which the strength of wrought iron is complemented by logs stacked along the wall, creating a contrast between the diversity of nature and the coldness of human construction.

MACBA also presents superb temporary exhibitions, lecture series, and concerts.

© MACBA

> **The MACBA Library**
> Exhibition catalogs, journals, contemporary music scores, and audio and audiovisual resources including sound art and video art are just some of the collections in the library.

Centre de Cultura Contemporània de Barcelona (CCCB)

🚇 *Catalunya, Universitat (L1, L2, L3). C. Montalegre 5. 93 306 41 00. www.cccb.org. Open Tue–Sun 11am–8pm (Thu 10pm). Closed Jan 1, Dec 25. €4.50 (free 1st Wed of the month, Thu 8–10pm, Sun 3–8pm).*

Part of MACBA, the CCCB and Center d'Estudis i Recursos Culturals occupy the old Casa de la Caritat (House of Charity, 18C). The building, renovated by the architects Helio Piñón and Albert Viaplana, includes an original decor design in its **patio★**, with sgraffito, mosaics, and floral motifs on the third. A huge glazed façade fills the fourth side of the courtyard.
The CCCB hosts conferences, temporary exhibitions, and events related to contemporary culture.

Centre d'Estudis i de Recursos Culturals

C. Montalegre 7. 93 402 25 65. Open Mon–Fri 9am–3pm.

As you go through the porch you will find the **Pati Manning** (18C), a harmonious design consisting of two floors of galleries on columns, also decorated with sgraffito and mosaics.

Museu d'Història de la Ciutat

©Gregory Wrona/APA Publications

Museu d'Història de la Ciutat★★

🅼 *Catalunya (L1, L3), Urquinaona (L1, L4), Liceu (L3), Jaume I (L4). Pl. del Rei, entrance on C. del Veguer. 93 256 21 00. www.museuhistoria. bcn.cat. Open Apr–Sept Tue–Sat 10am–8pm; Oct–Mar Tue–Sat 10am–2pm, 4–7pm; year-round Sun and public holidays 10am–8pm. Closed Jan 1, May 1, Jun 24, Dec 25. €7 (free Sun after 3pm).*

This museum takes you on a fascinating underground tour that covers the entire site before reaching the Palau Reial Major.

Roman and Visigoth Barcelona★★★

The Roman and Visigoth city lies hidden beneath the Plaça del Rei. This is an eerie walk among large sections of walls, streets, houses, shops, and workshops of the Roman period. The remains include a salting factory, a laundry, and a winery (recognizable by its many amphorae), along with a whole panoply relating to the bishops of Visigoth Barcelona. The underground trail leads to two barrel-vaulted Romanesque rooms that were part of the former Counts' Palace. Here there are some sculptures, inscriptions, and busts dating from the 1C to 4C. Farther on, the Jaume I Room contains large 13C Gothic murals discovered in 1998.

Palau Reial Major – The palace was the home of the counts of Barcelona before becoming the residence of the kings of Aragon, who generally preferred to live outside the city. The building, whose construction began in the 11C and 12C on the remains of the Roman wall, continued to expand until it reached its current size in the late 14C. In the 16C one wing was occupied by the Tribunal of the Inquisition, and the accused were tried in the interior courtyard. The façade has a monumental structure, with large, recessed, surbased arches produced by the conjunction of buttresses.

Today, the Museu Frederic Marès (see p 82) occupies part of the building, which between the 1940s and 1970 was restored and remodeled for the purpose.

Saló del Tinell – Built between 1359 and 1362, this is a huge hall some 56ft/17m high, its roof supported on both sides by six semicircular monumental arches. Tradition has it that this is the banqueting hall in which the Catholic kings received the explorer Christopher Columbus in 1493, on his first return from America.

Capella de Santa Àgata★★ – This palatine chapel, decorated with polychrome wood, was built by Jaume II in the 14C on the site of an earlier Romanesque chapel. It was dedicated to St Agatha in the 17C.

Don't miss

◆ The magnificent **Constable's altarpiece**★★ (1465) by Jaume Huguet, commissioned by the Constable, Peter of Portugal, depicts scenes from the life of the Virgin Mary and Jesus. Note the Adoration of the Magi, one of the dominant themes of Catalan painting, on the central panel and, on the upper section, a Calvary.

Mirador del Rei Martí – This tower offers an unrivaled **view**★★ of the entire old city, dominated by the dome of La Mercè at the bottom.

Museu d'Arqueològia de Catalunya★

Ⓜ *Espanya (L1, L3), Poble Sec (L3). Pg de Santa Madrona 39–41, Parc de Montjuic. 93 423 21 49. www.mac.cat. Open Tue–Sat 9.30am–7pm, Sun and public holidays 10am–2.30pm. Closed Jan 1 & 6, Dec 25–26. €3 (free last Sun of the month, Apr 23, May 18, Sept 11 & 24). The museum is currently being reorganized and some rooms may be closed to visitors.*

Created in 1935 at the instigation of the famous archeologist **Pere Bosch Gimpera** (1891–1974), it traces the history of Catalonia through its exhibits: Paleolithic, Neolithic, Bronze Age, Iron Age, Greek and Phoenician settlements, Roman culture, the Visigoth period, and finally, the Middle Ages. The objects displayed (tools, amphora, mosaics, and votive sculptures) are

©Gregory Wrona/APA Publications

Museu d'Arqueología de Catalunya

Royal galley of Don John of Austria in the Museu Marítim

J. Balanya/Michelin

typical of each particular period. Besides a library of 40,000 volumes, it also houses an **experimental workshop for the blind**, teaching the tactile recognition of archeological material.

In addition to the museum in Barcelona, there are branches complete with archeological sites and a museum or interpretive center in Empúries, Olèrdola, Girona (Monastir de Sant Pere de Galligants and underwater sites), and Ullastret.

Museu Marítim★

Ⓜ *Drassanes. Av. de les Drassanes. 93 342 99 20. www.mmb.cat. Open daily 10am–8pm. Closed Jan 1 & 6, Dec 25–26. €2.50.*

In a superb setting, this museum offers a fascinating tour through the history of the Catalan navy and holds many valuable items. In addition to ships and figure-heads, in the section devoted to mapping you can see the Portolan of Gabriel de Vallseca (1439), a nautical map of the Mediterranean that belonged to Amerigo Vespucci. The vast central nave contains a spectacular life-size

replica of the **royal galley of Don John of Austria★★**, the ship that led the Christian forces at Lepanto (October 7, 1571) and was built here. It is full of carved ornamentation and allegorical paintings. The entry ticket includes a visit to the **Santa Eulàlia pailebot**. This three-masted vessel (1918) is anchored at Moll de Bosch i Alsina, in Port Vell, beyond the Rambla de Mar.

CaixaForum

Ⓜ *Espanya (L1, L3). Marqués de Comillas 6–8 (corner of C. de Mèxic). 93 476 86 30. www.laCaixa.es/ ObraSocial. Open daily 10am– 8pm (Sat 10pm). No charge.*

"La Caixa" Foundation's cultural center, housed in a building in Montjuïc designed by **Josep Puig i Cadafalch** *(see Architects)*, provides an unusual backdrop for prestigious temporary exhibitions in addition to its collections on the themes of other cultures, sculpture, architecture, photography, and painting. There is an auditorium where performances of music and dance are staged, a cinema, and a library.

Don't miss

♦ The permanent installation by **Joseph Beuys**, *Espacio de dolor* (1983). In a lead-lined room lit by a single bulb, two silver rings are suspended from the ceilng, one apparently representing an adult, the other a child—you are encouraged to come up with your own interpretation.

Design Hub Barcelona (DHUB)

Ⓜ *Palau Reial (L3). Palau de Pedralbes, Av. Diagonal 686. 93 256 34 65. www.dhub-bcn.cat. Open Tue–Sun 10am–6pm (public holidays 3pm). Closed Jan 1, Jun 24, Dec 25–26. €5 including admission to DHUB Montcada (free Sun 3–8pm and 1st Sun of the month).*

Established by the Cultural Institute of Barcelona, the **Design Hub Barcelona (DHUB)** is intended for the study and promotion of knowledge in decorative arts and design. The Palau de Pedralbes houses the Museu de les Arts Decoratives and Museu Tèxtil i d'Indumentària, along with the Gabinet de les Arts Gràfiques, which organizes exhibitions. The building also houses the Museu de Ceràmica.

Museu de les Arts Decoratives★

–1st level. Rich and very diverse collections (furniture, clocks, carriages, wallpaper, etc), it offers a tour entitled "From the one-off objects to product design" taking in everyday objects, from medieval times to the present (the Modernist period is particularly well represented). Cabinets, desks, chairs, lamps, chests, and bottles offer an idea of changing customs and habits, as well as technological breakthroughs.

Museu Tèxtil i d'Indumèntaria

– The museum has a permanent exhibition entitled "Dressing the body", a trip through the world of fashion from the 16C to the present day. Here you can see the creations of Spanish (Balenciaga, Paco Rabanne) and international (Dior, Lagerfeld) fashion designers.

Museu de Ceràmica

Ⓜ *Palau Reial (L3). Palau de Pedralbes, Av. Diagonal 686. 93 256 34 65. www.museuceramica. bcn.es. Open Tue–Sun 10am–6pm, (public holidays 3pm). Closed Jan 1, May 1, Jun 24, Dec 25–26. €5 including admission to Museu de les Arts Decoratives and Museu Tèxtil i d'Indumèntaria (free 1st Sun of the month).*

The Museum of Ceramics displays its collection on a rotating basis. Highlights include Catalan and Valencian productions, including 18C and 19C examples from Alcora.

Don't miss

♦ Works of Catalan ceramist **Josep Llorens Artigas**, displayed alongside those of Picasso and Miró in the modern section.

©Disseny Hub Barcelona

Design Hub Barcelona

ARTISTS

Every artist needs inspiration and Barcelona certainly has the power to inspire creative endeavor. Picasso, Miró, Dalí, Tàpies, and Marès all have local connections and are recognized in museums and foundations bearing their name. The artists' own works are on display, but some of their collections are also not to be missed, from the art that influenced Miró to Marès' irresistible Cabinet of Curiosities.

PICASSO

Born in Málaga on October 25, 1881, Pablo Picasso began drawing at a very young age. His father, himself a professor of art, recognized and encouraged his talent. In 1895 his family relocated to Barcelona, where Picasso went on to study at La Llotja, the School of Fine Arts. A co-founder of the Cubist movement, along with Georges Braque, Picasso's unique and diverse style evolved continually throughout his career and challenged the definitions of what art could be. Not surprisingly, his eccentric lifestyle attracted as much attention as his art.

Museu Picasso★★

Ⓜ *Arc de Triomp (L1), Liceu (L3), Jaume I (L4). C. de Montcada 15–23. 93 256 30 00. www.museupicasso. bcn.es. Open Tue–Sun 10am–8pm. Closed Jan 1, May 1, Jun 24, Dec 25–26. €9 including temporary exhibition, €5.80 temporary exhibition only.*

A testimony to the relationship between the artist and Barcelona, this museum pays tribute to Picasso in the city where he developed as an artist and where he lived from 1895 until his departure for Paris in 1903.

The section dealing with the artist in his youth is truly remarkable. There are drawings from his childhood, free exercises, and academically inspired works: *La Première Communion (The First Communion)* (1896) and *Science et Charité (Science and Charity)* (1897).

It has several interesting items from the **Blue Period**, including *Los Desamparados (The Helpless)* (1903) and *El Loco (The Madman)* (1904). The **Las Meninas★** series comprises 58 paintings, a passionate reflection based on the Velázquez work of that name. The collection is rounded off by various paintings on the theme of doves

Courtyard of Museu Picasso

©Turespaña

MUST SEE

Cubism

The term "Cubism" was coined by Louis Vauxcelles, a French art critic. It refers to the revolutionary Cubist Movement pioneered in the early 20C by Picasso and his friend and fellow artist Georges Braque. This highly distinctive style, which presents the subject in the form of two-dimensional geometrical shapes emphasized by color or the use of light and shade, became progressively more abstract as Picasso and Braque advanced the technique. One of the most influential art styles of the early 20C, Cubism was adopted and further developed by many painters that followed.

as symbols of peace and freedom, a few landscapes, and several other significant works: *Portrait of Jacqueline, Piano,* and *Harlequin.*

OUT & ABOUT

Centre Picasso d'Orta★

43596 Horta de Sant Joan. 977 43 53 30. www.centrepicasso.org. Open Jul & Aug Tue–Sun 11am–2pm (Sat also 5–8pm); rest of year 11am–1.30pm (Sat also 5–8pm). Times vary on public holidays. €3.

The Centre Picasso is located in Horta, where Picasso spent the summers of 1898 and 1909 and of which he declared that every-thing he knew, he had learned in Horta. It was on the second visit, when he was accompanied by Fernande Olivier, his mistress and model, that Picasso began to experiment with the artistic style that was to become known as Cubism. Housed in a 16C hospital building, the gallery exhibits reproductions of the works created by Picasso during his time in the town, along with drawings and sketches. Temporary exhibitions relating to the artist are also held.

JOAN MIRÓ

Joan Miró was a painter, sculptor, and ceramist born in Barcelona in 1893. The son of a watchmaker

Centre Picasso d'Orta

and goldsmith, Miró was creating his art from as young as eight years old. He decided to dedicate his life to painting after surviving a serious bout of typhoid fever in 1911. Despite being firmly associated with the Surrealist movement, Miró did not apply this definition to his work as he felt that to do so would suppress his freedom to experiment. He died in Palma de Mallorca in 1983.

Fundació Joan Miró★★★

Ⓜ *Paral.lel (L2, L3), then funicular. Parc de Montjuïc. 93 443 94 70. www.bcn.fjmiro.es. Open Jul–Sept Tue–Sat 10am–8pm (Thu 9.30pm); Oct–Jun Tue–Sat 10am–7pm; year-round Sun and public holidays 10am–2.30pm. €8.50, €4 temporary exhibitions only.*

The **building**★★ that houses the foundation given to the city by Joan Miró was built in 1971 by **Josep Lluís Sert** (1902–83), a personal friend of the painter. This is one of the most beautiful works of rationalism throughout the Mediterranean. Its architecture is characterized by open space both inside and outside, seeking a balance between landscape and building. The treatment of light, which penetrates vertically into the rooms through large skylights, emphasizes this approach. In 1988, Jaume Freixa extended the building in line with the original design of Sert.

The collection, established by Miró himself, contains more than 10,000 works, including paintings, sculptures, collages, drawings, and graphic works. It allows you to appreciate the development of the artist, influenced at first by Realism and later by Surrealism. After the terrible works inspired by the Spanish Civil War and World War II that followed it, there is a display of Miró's calm and light final period. A visit is rounded off with a small collection of contemporary art, created a year after the artist's death, representing a tribute to Miró by artists such as Chillida, Saura, Duchamp, Max Ernst, and Rauschenberg.

Since 1990 the Foundation has exhibited **Mercury Fountain**★ by Alexander Calder, created in 1937 for the Spanish Pavilion of the Universal Exhibition in Paris, an allusion to Almadén, the town

Fundació Joan Miró

Parc Joan Miró

© Gregory Wrona/APA Publications

containing the world's largest mercury mines and one of the places most affected by the Spanish Civil War.

Finally, there is a pleasant **sculpture garden** containing works by young Catalan artists. The Foundation also organizes exhibitions of contemporary art.

Parc Joan Miró

Ⓜ *Espanya (L1), Tarragona (L3). C. de Tarragona/C. Aragó 2. www.bcn.cat/parcsijardins. Open daily May–Sept 10am–9pm (Mar & Nov 7pm, Apr & Oct 8pm, Dec–Feb 6pm). No charge.*

Known as the "Escorxador" (the Abattoir), this expansive park is built on the site of a former municipal slaughterhouse. The park was created on two levels—the lower is landscaped with palms, pines, fragrant eucalyptus trees, and colorful flowers. The upper level is paved and the main focus of interest is a huge phallic sculpture by Joan Miró called *Dona i ocell* (*Woman and Bird*), which rises 72ft/22m above a small pool. Located in the nearby Plaça Braus Las Arenas is a former bullfighting ring. Opened in 1900, it was earmarked for a revamp by the Richard Rodgers Partnership to turn it into a leisure center. Unfortunately, the promoters of the venture have gone bankrupt, so the site has been closed.

Surrealism

Although the words "Surrealism" and "Dalí" tend to go hand in hand, this method of expressing the workings of the subconscious mind actually began as a literary movement in the aftermath of World War I and was then adopted by a number of artists before Salvador Dalí took it to a new and even more bizarre level. Since the absence of any form of inhibition is the key to Surrealism, Joan Miró made a good point in not wishing the Surrealist "label" to be applied to his own work.

ARTISTS

SALVADOR DALÍ

Salvador Felipe Jacinto Dalí I Domènech was born in Figueres in 1904. Although he attended the Academy of Fine Arts in Madrid, he held his first one-man show in Barcelona in 1925. He became known internationally when three of his paintings were shown at the 1928 Carnegie International Exhibition in Pittsburg. The following year he joined the Surrealist movement and also met Gala Eluard (wife to poet Paul Eluard), who was to become his lover, muse, and manager. Dalí was a unique, flamboyant, and eccentric character known as much for his unusual methods of self-promotion as for his craft, earning him the derogatory anagrammatic nickname "Avida Dollars." Dalí died in January 1989 in the tower of his own museum, aged 84.

DalíBarcelona

Ⓜ *Jaume 1 (L4). C. Arcs 5. 93 318 17 74. www.dalibarcelona.com. Open daily 10am–10pm. €8.*

DalíBarcelona

The headquarters of the Real Círculo Artístico museum of Barcelona, the Pignatelli Palace houses the permanent **DalíBarcelona** collection on two levels. In this slightly crowded venue, you will see 44 sculptures produced by the artist in the 1970s, including the *Cosmic Elephant* (1974). All this is accompanied by preparatory drawings and watercolors, ceramics, numerous photos of the artist, and the model of the "falla" (a piece intended to be burned), which he produced for the festival of Valencia in 1954.

OUT & ABOUT

Casa-Museu Salvador Dalí★★

Portlligat, Cadaqués. 97 225 10 15. www.salvador-dali.org/museus/portlligat. Open daily mid-Jun–mid-Sept 9.30am–9pm; mid-Feb–mid-Jun and mid-Sept–Jan 6 Tue–Sun 10.30am–6pm. Closed Jan 1, Jan 6–mid-Feb, Dec 25. €10. Advance booking required.

The Portlligat House-Museum was Dalí's home from 1930, when the house was little more than a hut, until the death of his wife and muse, Elena Diakonova (Gala), in 1982, when Dalí moved to Púbol Castle. Over the years, Dalí extended the house in labyrinthine fashion, each new room being given a window that framed Portlligat Bay. The house is packed with mementoes of Dalí and provides a fascinating insight into all aspects of his life.

Alan Moore/Michelin

MUST SEE

Teatre-Museu Dalí★★

Gala-Salvador Dalí Square 5, Figueres. 97 267 75 00. www.salvador-dali.org/museus/ figueres. Open Mar–May Tue–Sun 9.30am–6pm; Jun daily 9.30am– 6pm; Jul–Sept daily 9am–8pm (Aug also 10pm–1am, see website); Oct Tue–Sun 9.30am–6pm; Nov–Feb Tue–Sun 10.30am–6pm. Closed Jan 1, Dec 25. €11 including Dalí Jewels exhibition.

Teatre-Museu Dalí, Figueres

©Turespaña

The extraordinary building in which the museum is housed is described as "the world's largest surrealist object." It was designed by Dalí himself and constructed in the early 1960s around the ruins of Figueres' municipal theater, which was destroyed by fire at the end of the Spanish Civil War in 1939. Inaugurated in 1974, the museum exhibits a range of works spanning Dalí's whole career (1904–89), including *The Girl from Figueres* (1926), *Soft Self-Portrait with Fried Bacon* (1941), and *Dawn, Noon, Afternoon and Evening* (1979). There are also works created by the artist specifically for the museum and a collection of works by other artists, including El Greco, Modest Urgell, and Antoni Pitxot.

Don't miss

◆ **Dalí Jewels** A collection of jewels in gold and precious stones, designed by Dalí between 1941 and 1970, together with drawings and paintings on cardboard of the designs. The collection is housed in an annex to the museum and can be visited separately *(entrance on corner between Ma Àngels Vayreda and La Pujada del Castell; opening times as for museum; €6).*

◆ **Mae West Room** Climb the ladder-like set of stairs by the wall to the viewing platform and look through the lens hung between the legs of a camel, and all will be revealed.

◆ **Palace of the Wind** With an impressive trompe l'oeil ceiling painting.

Casa-Museu Castell Gala Dalí★

Pl. Gala Dalí, Puból-la-Pera. 97 248 86 55. www.salvador-dali.org/ museus/pubol. Open daily mid-Jun–mid-Sept 10am–8pm; mid-Mar–mid-Jun and mid-Sept–Oct 10am–6pm; Nov–Dec 10am–5pm. Closed Jan–mid-Mar and public holidays, Dec 25. €7.

The Gala Dalí Castle dates from the late 14C/early 15C. When Dalí bought it in 1969 as a sanctuary for Gala, its poor state of repair lent the building a romantic air, which Dalí was careful to retain. The restored castle still has an austere medieval feel, and even includes a throne for Gala, mounted on a little dais.

ARTISTS

ANTONI TÀPIES

Antoni Tàpies, born in Barcelona in 1923 into a nationalist Catalan family, began his career as a Surrealist painter and graphic artist with no formal training. He made his mark working in mixed media, creating textured paints and adding anything from string to bits of furniture to his artworks. Tàpies' work has always been influenced by current political and social events, and he encourages other artists to be spontaneous and to steer away from tradition. Tàpies lives in Barcelona.

Fundació Antoni Tàpies★★

Ⓜ *Pg de Gràcia (L3, L4). C. Aragó 255. 93 487 03 15. www.fundaciotapies.org. Open Tue–Sun 10am–8pm. Closed Jan 1 & 6, Dec 25–26. €7.*

Created by the artist in 1984, this foundation is housed in the Modernist building of the former publishing company **Editorial Montaner i Simón** *(see p 71)*, which is the work of Lluís Domènech i Montaner. On top of the façade of this imposing red-brick building is a large sculpture of aluminum cables by Tàpies.

Núvol i cadira (Cloud and Chair) is the emblem of the foundation, representing the symbolic universe of the artist. The interior, consisting of two main levels and a basement, is a large space lit by natural overhead light through its dome and pyramidal roof. Displayed on a rotation basis, the museum's holdings, mostly works bequeathed to it by Tàpies, are the most comprehensive collection of his work and illustrate his artistic journey since 1948.

Notice in particular the fabrics used in the famous *serie matérica*, where Tàpies explored the medium of paper murals as a mirror or metaphor of the time. The expressiveness of the rough surface is highlighted by the symbols the artist has introduced (a piece of paper and various letters). Various shades of color are added to the crevices and folds of the material to produce a dramatic atmosphere. The library, which has retained the wooden shelves of the publishing house, has a large collection of documents on 20C art, documents concerning the work of Tàpies, and a large section devoted to Oriental culture and arts that influenced the work of the painter so profoundly.

Fundació Antoni Tàpies

FREDERIC MARÈS

Frederic Marès i Deulovol was born in Portbou in 1893 and in 1903 moved with his family to Barcelona, where he later trained as a sculptor at the School of Fine Arts. His early work was mainly portraits, funeral sculptures, and female nudes, but after the Spanish Civil War he focused his attention on restoring monuments, as well as creating commemorative and religious sculpture. Marès was also an avid collector of almost anything he could get his hands on and today his collection is on display in three locations, one in the city and two outside. Marès died in 1991 at the age of 98.

© Museu Frederic Marès/Ramon Muro

Museu Frederic Marès

Museu Frederic Marès★

Ⓜ *Jaume 1 (L4). Pl. de Sant Iu 5–6. 93 256 35 00. www.museumares. bcn.es. The museum is currently closed for renovations and will reopen in 2011; in the meantime, interactive panels are installed in the courtyard (open Tue–Sun 10am–10pm).*

Frederic Marès' incredible collections are on display in three separate locations. Two are located outside the city (at Arenys de Mar and Montblanc). This one is in the outbuildings of the Palau Reial Major. The museum's collection is divided into two sections:

Sculpture section – Occupying two floors and the crypt of the palace, it consists of major works of Spanish sculpture, arranged chronologically. Note the impressive **collection★** of wooden polychrome crucifixes and Calvary scenes (12C–14C) and of Roman-esque and Gothic depictions of the **Virgin and Child★**, a 16C **Laying in the Tomb★**, containing six characters, and **The Calling of St Peter★**, a 12C marble produced by the Master of Cabestany, a Catalan sculptor who worked mainly in Languedoc and Roussillon. You can admire the unique expressions on their faces, with oval eyes that seem to leap out of their sockets.

Gabinete del Coleccionista – This so-called Cabinet of Curiosities is really striking, displaying the results of the relentless endeavors of its indefatigable collector. It will almost render you speechless. Thousands of items from daily life, arranged thematically, are laid out in these vast halls: fans, jewelry, combs, gloves, pipes, tobacco pouches, packs of cards, canes, watches, earrings, rosaries, china, admission and transport tickets, ancient cameras… They constitute a little museum of everyday objects, from the humblest to the most valuable. Finally, you can also make a visit to the artist's studio.

PARKS AND GARDENS

With its beautiful Mediterranean climate, Barcelona boasts a wide variety of parks, ranging from large, open, landscaped green spaces to the smaller, more intimate, former private gardens and parklands of the city's nobility. Many of these parks are adorned with land art and sculpture by the city's finest artists, and all make an ideal place to escape the bustling streets and take some time to relax.

Parc de la Ciutadella★

Ⓜ *Arc de Triomf (L1). Pg de Picasso 1. www.bcn.cat/parcsi jardins. Open daily 10am–dusk.*

Following Barcelona's long resistance to his siege in 1714, Felipe V had a citadel built in 1715 to keep the city under control. The construction involved the demolition of more than a thousand houses in La Ribera. The Citadel became, like the castle of Montjuïc, a symbol of the city's repression. Its demolition occurred following the liberal revolution of 1868, being subsequently replaced by a public park in which the Universal Exhibition of 1888 was held.

The entrance, **Passeig de Lluís Companys**, is a broad avenue leading to the heart of the park from the **Arc de Triomf**, the gateway to the Exhibition.

Highlights include:

Castell dels Tres Dragons★★
see Architects

Cascada★ – Built with the assistance of the young Gaudí, this gigantic waterfall is at the forefront of a large circular square. Right next door is a pond where you can rent boats.

Hivernacle i Umbracle – These are two greenhouses, one made of glass and iron, the other of brick and wood. The former has been converted into a café.

Plaça de Armes – This rectangular landscaped area in the center

Parc de la Ciutadella

©Turespaña

of the park contains the only remains of the **fortress**, its arsenal, a beautiful Baroque building, currently home to the Parliament of Catalonia. In the square lies an oval pond in the center of which is the famous sculpture *Desconsol (Sorrow)* by Josep Llimona.

Jardí Botánic

Ⓜ *Espanya (L1, L3).*
C. Dr Font i Quer 2. 93 256 41 60. www.jardibotanicbcn.es. Open daily Nov–Jan 10am–5pm; Feb, Mar & Oct 10am–6pm; Apr, May & Sept 10am–7pm; Jun–Aug 10am–8pm. Closed Jan 1, Dec 25. €3.50 (free Sun 3–8pm and last Sun of the month).

This delightful botanical garden contains a remarkable collection of over 2,000 plants gathered from the Mediterranean region. The garden was created in the last decade of the 20C on a steeply sloping site, transforming the area from a run-down neighborhood to a tranquil place with fine views.

Jardins de Joan Maragall

Ⓜ *Espanya (L1, L3). Av. de l'Estadi. www.bcn.cat/parcsijardins. Open weekends and public holidays 10am–3pm.*

These peaceful gardens surround a small royal residence, built for King Alfonso XIII in 1929 within the enclosure of the International Exhibition. The gardens are formal in design, with avenues, lawns, parterres, flights of steps, ponds, and ornamental fountains. Scattered around the garden are 32 sculptures, each by a different artist and dating mainly from the

© Turespaña
Jardí Botànic

second half of the 20C. One of these, Ernest Maragall's *Allegoria de la Sardana*, honors the traditional Cátalan dance.

Jardins de Mossèn Cinto Verdaguer

Ⓜ *Drassanes (L3), Paral·el (L3). C. dels Tarongers 1–5, main entrance on Av. de Miramar. www.bcn.cat/parcsijardins. Open daily May–Sept 10am–9pm; Mar & Nov 10am–7pm; Apr & Oct 10am–8pm; Dec–Feb 10am–6pm.*

This garden, created on the site of an old stone quarry, forms part of the Parc de Montjuïc and is one of the most colorful and beautiful in the city. It is especially attractive in early spring, when the bulb plants are in bloom, and again at the height of summer. A number of small ponds, arranged on either side of a flight of steps, are planted with aquatic species. The gardens are named in honor of the Catalan poet Jacint Verdaguer (1845–1902)—look out for Ramon Sabi's sculpture *Noia dels lliris* (1970), with its inscription of Verdaguer's verses.

Parc de Cervantes

©Turespaña

Jardins de Mossèn Costa i Llobera

Ⓜ *Drassanes (L3), Paral·lel (L3). Ctra. de Miramar 1. Open daily 10am–9pm.*

This is the largest exotic garden in Barcelona, with a vast range of species of tropical and subtropical plants. In among the cacti are Ros i Bofarull's sculpture *L'au dels temporals*; Txell Duran's monolith honoring the Catalan cactologist Joan Pañella, who created the gardens along with the architect Joaquim Maria Casamor; and Viladomat's bronze figure *La Puntaire*.

Parc de Cervantes

Ⓜ *Zona Universitària (L3). Av. Diagonal 706. www.bcn.cat/ parcsijardins. Open daily May– Sept 10am–9pm; Mar & Nov 10am– 7pm; Apr & Oct 10am–8pm; Dec– Feb 10am–6pm.*

Extending beyond the university area, this gently sloping 9-acre/6ha park is home to a large **rose garden** *(roserar)* covering almost half of its area. No fewer than 220 varieties are represented, with a total of some 10,000 roses. Definitely a place for lovers! To see it at its best, visit the park between April and November. It is an ideal place to go for a walk, a bicycle ride, or even, as many in Barcelona do, for a run.

Parc de Collserola

Road from Vallvidrera to Sant Cugat, access by funicular, Peu del Funicular station.

This large area (20,000 acres/ 8,000ha), one of the high spots of the city, is ideal for a stroll to get away from it all. It's also an excellent location for cycling.

Parc de la Creueta del Coll

Ⓜ *Vallcarca (L3). Pg Mare de Déu del Coll 77. www.bcn.cat/parcsi jardins. Open daily May–Sept 10am–9pm; Mar & Nov 10am– 7pm; Apr & Oct 10am–8pm; Dec–Feb 10am–6pm.*

This disused quarry has become a park with a lake, where you can swim in summer beneath a large sculpture by Chillida entitled *Elogio del Agua (In Praise of Water)*.

Parc de l'Espanya Industrial

Ⓜ *Sants-Estació (L3, L5). Muntadas 1–37. www.bcn.cat/parcsijardins. Open daily May–Sept 10am–9pm; Mar & Nov 10am–7pm; Apr & Oct 10am–8pm; Dec–Feb 10am–6pm.*

Located west of the Sants Estació station, this area was created between 1982 and 1985 on a former industrial wasteland. In the lower part of this area, there is a boating pond. The upper esplanade has a series of metal sculptures recalling the city's industrial past, which is now in a state of decay.

©Turespaña

Parc de l'Espanya Industrial

Parc del Castell de l'Oreneta

Bus 66. C. Montevideo 45. www.bcn.cat/parcsijardins. Open daily May–Sept 10am–9pm; Mar & Nov 10am–7pm; Apr & Oct 10am–8pm; Dec–Feb 10am–6pm.

Castell de l'Oreneta Park lies at the foot of the Sant Pere Màrtir peak in the Collserola Mountains. It was created from two rural estates, one belonging to the family of Count Milà (Can Bonavia) and one to the Tous family, who built the now ruined castle (1910) that gives the park its name. The area is planted with a wide variety of trees, including pines and fruit trees, as well as fragrant herbs such as thyme and lavender. A highlight is the miniature train, which operates on Sundays between 11am and 2pm.

Parc del Laberint d'Horta

Ⓜ *Mundi (L3). Pg dels Castanyers 1. www.bcn.cat/parcsijardins. Open daily May–Sept 10am–9pm; Mar & Nov 10am–7pm; Apr & Oct 10am–8pm; Dec–Feb 10am–6pm.*

Located at the foot of Collserola, the Laberint d'Horta is an old 18C estate containing a beautiful house built for the Marquis of Alfarràs in accordance with the eclectic tastes of the period. The park, decorated with carvings of mythological figures, niches, and features of Arab origin, has a bucolic labyrinth of cypress trees.

Parc Estació del Nord

Ⓜ *Arc de Triomf, Marina (L1). C. Nàpols 70. Open daily May–Sept 10am–9pm; Mar & Nov 10am–7pm; Apr & Oct 10am–8pm; Dec–Feb 10am–6pm.*

Occupying an area around the former railway station Estació del Nord, the main feature of this small but popular park is a piece of land art by New York artist Beverly Pepper. The sweeping and contoured shapes are covered with pieces of blue and white glazed ceramic tiles, reminiscent of Gaudí's smashed-tile technique.

Parc Güell★★ – *See Architects*
Parc Joan Miró – *See Artists*

PARKS AND GARDENS

EXCURSIONS

If the hustle and bustle of the big city gets too much, you can always take a trip out into the countryside around Barcelona. Here you'll find stunning coastlines, picture-postcard fishing ports, resorts with sandy beaches and fascinating architecture, breathtaking scenery, historic towns, and pretty villages perched on mountainous crags. Certainly worth a detour!

AROUND BARCELONA

Monestir de Sant Cugat del Vallès★★

Claustre del Monestir, Sant Cugat del Vallès. 11mi/18km northwest of Barcelona via the BP1417. 93 675 99 51. www.museu.santcugat. cat. Open Tue–Sat 10am–1.30pm, 3–7pm (Jun–Sept 3–8pm), Sun and public holidays 10am–2.30pm. Closed Jan 1 & 6, Dec 25–26. €3 (free with guided tour at noon, 1st Sunday of the month).

Octagonal dome of the monastery church

© www.monestirs.cat

This former **Benedictine abbey** is located in the heart of the town to which it gave its name. This ancient Roman camp became famous because St Cucufat (Cugat) and his companions were martyred here. They were put to death during the final persecution of Roman emperor Diocletian. Monastic buildings were built on the tomb of the martyr, between the 12C and 14C and these were originally fortified. From the ancient abbey buildings there now remain the church (now the parish church), the cloister, and the chapter house, which has been converted into a chapel (Capella del Santissím, the Chapel of the Blessed Sacrament). The former abbey palace is a Gothic building rebuilt in the 18C, which now houses education offices.

Church★ – Built in the 12C, this sanctuary with three naves and three semicircular apses is a magnificent example of the transition between Romanesque and Gothic. The oldest part of the church is the tower (11C), decorated with Lombard strips. The lantern tower, erected at the transept, and the octagonal dome that covers it reflect an evolution of the original style. Other changes were

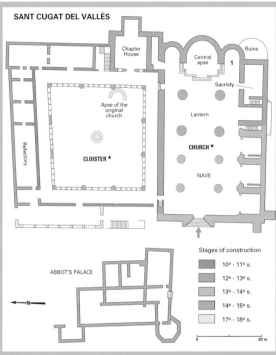

SANT CUGAT DEL VALLÈS

Chapter House

Central apse

Ruins

1

Sacristy

Apse of the original church

Lantern

CHURCH ★

Refectory

CLOISTER ★

NAVE

ABBOT'S PALACE

← N →

Stages of construction

10e - 11e s.
12e - 13e s.
13e - 14e s.
14e - 15e s.
17e - 18e s.

0   20 m

made, including the addition of three side chapels.

The smooth façade, which is crowned with crenellations and consolidated buttresses, was completed shortly before 1350. A large circular rose window contrasts with the archivolts of the door. Worth noting inside is the beautiful **All Saints altarpiece★**, dating from the 14C, on which, following a Marian theme, the artist, Pere Serra, has managed to produce a series of dynamic and expressive characters.

Cloister★ – This is one of the largest Romanesque cloisters (11C–12C), with its 144 columns enclosing the garden. Note

especially the beautiful **capitals★** of the artist Arnau Cadell, connected in pairs by a single abacus. Several ornamental styles are developed here: the Corinthian (with acanthus leaves and geometrical figures), the figurative (birds, mermaids, and fantasy animals), and the historical perspective (biblical scenes and scenes of everyday life). The most interesting is the pillar in the northeast corner, where the sculptor has represented himself at work and has carved his name. In the second half of the 16C, an upper gallery was added, with beautiful Tuscan columns supporting semicircular arches.

Sant Joan Despí★

10mi/17km west of Barcelona via the B10-N11.

In the suburbs of Barcelona, on the main highway connecting Madrid to the capital of Catalonia, Sant Joan Despí became one of the favored resorts of Barcelona's wealthy élite at the turn of the 19C and 20C. To this day many Modernist houses from the period remain, grouped in the center of the town.

At Nos. 28 and 30 Jacint Verdaguer *(to the east of the church)*, **Casa Unifamilial** is a house with an asymmetrical façade decorated with predominantly green mosaics and topped off with four fruits, just like those found at the Sagrada Família in Barcelona.

Directly opposite lies the **Casa Rovira**, designed by the architect **Josep Maria Jujol i Gibert** (1879–1949), which is unfortunately in poor condition. The whole effect is somewhat classical in style, with religious images carved on the pediment.

Opposite, the **Torre Serra Xaus** is the work of the same architect.

From the original façade there emerges a massive square tower with red and blue patterns, depicting mythical bird and floral motifs. Across the road, the building is echoed by the **Jujol villa** (1932), a small house with a seaside feel and a garden containing tall palms.

Plaça de Catalunya seems overwhelmed by the **Casa Can Negre★★**, probably the most outstanding work by Jujol in Sant Joan Despí. Built between 1915 and 1930, it now houses the Jujol Study Center. The influence of Gaudí is apparent, with small blue mosaic benches similar to those of **Parc Güell★★** *(see p 66)*, and undulating shapes calling to mind the marine world. Note the rows of bony, wrought-iron arches supporting the balcony.

Farther north, in the Passeig de Canales, **Casa Aurigae★**, designed by the architect **Ignasi Mas i Morell** (1881–1953), uses the same type of decorative style as the Casa Rovira. The roof has a large brightly colored terrace. The **Torre de la Creu★**, once again a distinctive work by Jujol,

Casa Can Negre

©Ajuntament de Sant Joan Despí

is even more amazing. This large tower, with its round smooth shapes, is overlooked by several levels of terracing decorated with mosaics and ironwork. Note the beautiful wrought-iron gate in the garden.

Go back downtown by making a detour via **Carrer Montjuïc** where many other building façades—especially Nos. 28, 26, and 20—recall the Modernist past of the city, with beautifully styled pediment features.

La Colònia Güell★

Santa Coloma de Cervelló. Leave Sant Joan Despí by the C245 in the direction of Sant Boi. Take the BV2002, then follow the directions to Colònia Güell.

The construction of Colònia Güell, declared a World Heritage Site by UNESCO in 2005, was begun in the late 19C around the town of **Santa Coloma de Cervelló**, at the instigation of Eusebi Güell. The industrialist was planning to build a modern textile mill there, replacing the one he already owned in Barcelona, and wanted to create a real working-class neighborhood including, besides the plant and its offices, houses, shops, cultural facilities, and a church. Many architects were asked to work on the project, specifically **Antoni Gaudí**, who was entrusted with building the **church** *(see Architects).*
Apart from the church, none of the buildings is open to visitors; however, an exhibition at the tourist office outlines the main stages in the development of the complex. A tour lasting approximately 30 minutes is also on offer.

Adam, Eve and the paradise tree, Church of Santa Maria de Barberà

©VWPics/Photoshot

Barberà del Vallès

13mi/21km north of Barcelona via the C31, then the C58 (take the N150 toward Barberà del Vallès) and 3mi/5km from Sant Cugat del Vallès.

The town of Barberà del Vallès is joined to the south with **Sabadell**, a city with an industrial past that has earned it the nickname "Catalan Manchester."

Church of Santa Maria de Barberà – *At the end of Ronda de Santa Maria, on Pl. del Milenario. 93 711 21 01. Ask for the key from the custodian.* Built in the 11C to a design incorporating a single nave and three apses, on the south transept there is a rectangular spire with a pyramidal roof. The decoration of the walls, consisting of arches and Lombard strips, adds a softer touch to the architectural effect of the column bosses. The paintings in the apse (12C and 13C), which display a high level of artistry and are in perfect condition, develop themes in specifically Romanesque style.

COSTA BRAVA★★★

Costa Brava —"rugged coast"— accurately describes the coastal area between Blanes and the French border. The powerful landscape, mild climate, crystal waters, bright skies, and charming settlements—which traditionally make their living from fishing and coral-hunting, and now tourism— are among the attractions of this region, the most famous along the Catalan coastline.

Highlights

Port of Roses

L. Campion/Michelin

+ **Beaches** In the region of La Selva—**Blanes**, **Lloret de Mar**, **Tossa**—the landscape is wild. The cliffs plunge vertically into the sea, forming little coves. The coast of Baix Empordà, from **Sant Feliu de Guíxols** to **Begur**, is stunningly beautiful, with clear blue-green waters. The most spectacular scenery is in the region of **Roses**, **Cadaquès**, and **El Port de la Selva**, with wide, sandy beaches.

+ **Harbors** A scene typical of the Costa Brava is that of moored boats, used either for leisure activities or for fishing—the sight of fishermen auctioning their catch is very entertaining.

+ **Picturesque villages** Each of the villages along the Costa Brava has something unique to offer. Among them, **Cadaqués**—a haunt of artists and bohemians—has a relaxed, cosmopolitan vibe *(see p 102)*, while the medieval village of **Peratallada** has a particular charm of its own *(see p 101)*.

Calella de Palafrugell

J. Malburet/Michelin

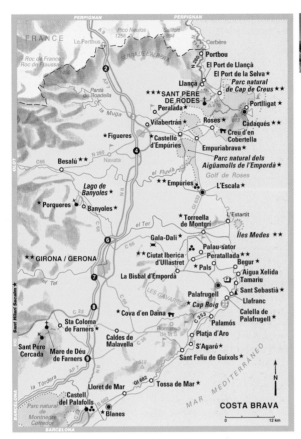

COSTA BRAVA

0   12 km

N

* **Gardens** An unexpected feature of the Costa Brava is the gardens—between Lloret de Mar and Blanes, for example, there are three major botanical gardens, all very different. Some of them offer spectacular views of parts of the coast that are otherwise not visible, including the botanical gardens of Cap Roig at **Calella de Palafrugell**, nestled on panoramic terraces overlooking the sea.

* **Ambience** There are countless ways to be entertained on the Costa Brava, but when you need a moment to catch your breath, there is always a quiet corner where you can recharge your batteries. The liveliest spot is Lloret de Mar, where the discos and bars remain open into the small hours, while open-air concerts and shows are staged on the beaches at Palamós, Sant Feliu de Guíxols, and Cadaqués.

Monestir de Sant Pere de Rodes★★★

97 238 75 59. www.mhcat.cat.
Open Tue–Sun. Closed Jan 1,
Dec 25–26.

On a steep slope of Mont Sant Salvador de Verdera, on a magnificent **site★★** against a backdrop of the Gulf of Lion and the Cap de Creus peninsula, stand the impressive ruins of a Benedictine monastery. Construction began in the 10C and its history is a veritable cloak-and-dagger saga featuring theft, fire, epidemics, and plunder.

The monastery is located on a small, irregular site, with the various buildings (church, cloister, and monastic lodgings) on different levels. At the highest point are the ruins of the **Castell de Sant Salvador de Verdera**. Nearby, the remains of the old village of Santa Creu de Rodes surround the **Iglesia de Santa Elena**.

Church★★ – This exceptional building is unique in Spanish medieval architecture. It displays an unusual uniformity, with distinct pre-Romanesque influences even though its construction dates to the 11C. Located on the north of the site, on a lower level than the other buildings, it has three naves. The central nave has a very high barrel vault, while the much narrower side aisles have semi-barrel vaults. The naves are separated by columns topped with superb **capitals★** decorated in Corinthian style with delicately sculpted acanthus leaves. The transept has two apsidal chapels and a central apse with a crypt and ambulatory.

Bell tower★★ – A magnificent example of 12C Lombard style, the square three-story bell tower (88ft/27m) lets in light through large arched openings.

Illes Medes★★

The tiny archipelago known as Illes Medes (53 acres/21.5ha in total), consisting of seven islets and some reefs, lies 0.6mi/1km off the coast of the Ampurdan. The scenery here is very beautiful, and the area is protected for its ecological richness, with a wide variety of species and ecosystems.

Monestir de Sant Pere de Rodes

R. Manent/Michelin

MUST SEE

Its karst formation has resulted in cavities and tunnels that form an ideal environment for marine flora and fauna—1,300 different species have been counted. This wealth of resources has long been exploited by fishermen and especially by coral-hunters, who since the 18C have extended their activities to take in the whole coastline.

Meda Gran – The largest of the islands displays a distinct lack of symmetry—its eastern coast consists of high limestone cliffs, while more erodible materials (clay, gypsum, and marl) form the gentle slopes of the west coast. Near the bay where the boats dock are two lighthouses; the newer of the two, built in 1930, is powered by solar energy.

Meda Petita – This islet is separated from Meda Gran by El Freuetó. The cliffs on the east coast are dotted with numerous caves and grottos.

Jardins de Santa Clotilde★★

Paratge de Santa Clotilde. 97 237 04 71. www.lloretdemar.org. Open Apr–Sept daily 10am–8pm, mid-Oct–Mar Tue–Sun 10am–5pm. Last admission 1hr before closing. Closed Jan 1 & 6, Dec 25. €4 (guided tour included Sat, Sun 10.30am).

These gardens, located on a clifftop at Lloret de Mar, are an oasis of tranquility, rare in this part of the Costa Brava. Restored in 2006, the gardens were set out in 1919 by the architect and landscape gardener Nicolau Maria Rubió i Tudurí (1891–1981),

View to Illes Medes

© Marlee/Bigstockphoto.com

a pupil of the French architect Jean-Claude Forestier. The owner, the Marquis of Roviralta, commssioned Rubió to design a garden inspired by those of the Italian Renaissance. You explore the terraced gardens by means of criss-cross paths and flights of brick steps. The trees are sparsely planted, allowing panoramic views of the coast and sea.

Peratallada★★

Built on rocky gullies, Peratallada—the name means "carved stone"—is considered to be one of the best examples of medieval architecture in the Ampurdan.

This fortified **village**, whose old alleys converge on the Plaça Major, clusters around the huge tower of the castle-fortress, today a luxury hotel. The **Plaça de les Voltes**, adorned with a small portico and lined with old houses, is one of the most emblematic images of the region.

Iglesia de Sant Esteve, an austere 13C building located outside the village, has a campanile typical of many churches in the region. The church is open to the public during masses.

101

CADAQUÉS★★

122mi/196km north of Barcelona on the A7 motorway. Turn off at junction 4. Cadaqués is signposted just before Roses.

Cadaques, a picturesque former fishing village nestling between clear blue sea and rocky mountains, is located on the south coast of the stunning Cap de Creus peninsula, which marks the point where the Pyrenees meet the Mediterranean. The shady, narrow streets and bohemian ambience attracted famous artists in the first half of the 20C and still lure many tourists today

Perafita road

Until the 19C the village of Cadaqués was completely isolated. It was finally linked to Roses by the construction of the **Perafita road★★**, with its photogenic views of the Ampurdan, the Gulf of Roses, the beautiful French coast, and the hills behind Cadaqués. The countryside around the town is a fabulous natural canvas, the gray tones of its rocks punctuated by green olive trees, and the mountains, terraced by slate walls, form a vast and impressive garden. A key feature of the area is the extraordinary light—Dalí said it made the mountains look as if Leonardo da Vinci had painted them. Visitors will take away memories of gleaming whitewashed houses, capricious winds, and the delicious seafood served in the local restaurants.

Museu de Geologìa

Pl. Dr Trèmols. 97 225 88 00.

Housed in a 19C casino, this museum displays different collections of geological materials found in the Comarca d'Alt Empordà region.

Santa Maria Church

C. del Portal de Mont. 97 225 83 15.

The shape of this 16C church has been immortalized by many painters and is a symbol of Cadaqués. It looks as if it is floating in the air. The exterior austerity contrasts with the interior, which houses a Baroque **retable★★** by Pau Costa. This work of art, a spectacular piece of gilded wood iconography, is one of the most remarkable of its kind in the region and was made by Joan Torras. The church also con-

---

Cadaqués' artists

From the late 19C many artists and intellectuals were drawn to Cadaqués. The Pitxot family of painters and musicians lived here, and Antoni Pitxot was a close friend and collaborator of Salvador Dalí, the greatest name associated with the town. Picasso completed the most famous of his Cubist works, *The Guitarist*, during a stay in 1910. The Surrealist painter Paul Eluard and his wife Gala (who later married Dalí) came to Cadaqués in the 1920s, and other visiting celebrities from the world of the arts included René Magritte, Luis Buñuel, Joan Miró, Federico García Lorca, Man Ray, and Marcel Duchamp.

MUST SEE

Cap de Creus lighthouse
Set among spectacular rocky outcrops, the Cap de Creus lighthouse is the most easterly point of the Iberian Peninsula. It was used as a location for the 1971 film *The Light at the Edge of the World*, starring Yul Brynner and Kirk Douglas. The amazing view can be enjoyed from the Restaurante Cap de Creus *(97 219 90 05; www. restaurantecapdecreus.com)*, located behind the lighthouse.

tains a chapel painted by Dalí. The popular **International Festival of Music** is also held here.

Parc Natural de Cap de Creus★★

2.5mi/4km north of Cadaqués.

Steep roads and paths lead to the Cap de Creus peninsula, offering some stunning contrasts on the way. One of the largest nature reserves in Catalonia, the park is divided into both maritime and land areas, making it Catalonia's first foreshore nature park. The rugged relief is criss-crossed by paths that will take you past sheer cliffs and hidden bays. Down on the seafront, little boats leave from El Port de La Selva and Cadaqués, taking visitors out to secluded creeks and inlets of great beauty. Much of the fauna and flora are rare or unique, and the park is a haven for walkers and bird-watchers. A lighthouse, built on the highest point of the park, offers panoramic **views★★★**.

Portlligat★

Just over a mile to the north of Cadaqués, this little bay was once a refuge for fisherman but today is home to pretty inlets and a delightful port. It owes its fame to Salvador Dalí, who had a house built here. The house is now a museum *(97 225 10 15; www. salvador-dali.org/museus/portl-ligat; open daily mid-Jun–mid-Sept 9.30am–9pm, open Tue–Sun mid-Feb–mid-Jun and mid-Sept–mid-Jan 10.30am–6pm; closed Jan 1, Jan 6–mid-Feb, Dec 25; 10€; advance booking required).*

Casa-Museu Salvador Dalí★★
see Artists

Picturesque village of Cadaqués

J. Malburet/Michelin

103

GIRONA★★

62mi/100km north of Barcelona on the A7 motorway.

Girona, a historic city at the confluence of the rivers Ter and Onyar, is the capital of the province of the same name. The old quarter, perched on a hilltop on the right bank of the Onyar, has a network of narrow, charming streets and impressive buildings. The new quarter lies between the left bank of the Onyar and Parc de la Devesa.

La Força Vella★★

Imposing buildings with fascinating architectural features and pleasant squares await you in the walled old quarter. The best way to explore the Força Vella is on foot. Wander through the narrow cobbled streets and twisting alleys; examine the gray stone buildings, and admire the Gothic cathedral. The historic district is home to many key museums and is a perfect place to spend a few hours before a bite to eat on the Rambla de la Llibertat.

Banys Àrabs★ – *C. Rei Ferran el Catòlic. 97 221 32 62. www.banys arabs.org. Open Apr–Sept Mon–Sat 10am–7pm, Sun 10am–2pm; Oct–Mar Mon–Sat 10am–2pm. €2 (for tour).* The Arab Baths were built in the 12C and include a caldarium (hot bath), frigidarium (cold bath), and tepidarium (somewhere in between!). Learn more about their history and use on the tour. No bathing, however.

Cathedral★ – *Pl. de la Catedral. 97 221 44 26. www.catedraldegirona. org. Open daily Apr–Oct 10am-8pm; Nov–Mar 10am-7pm. Nave closed during services. €5, €3 when nave closed (free on Sun).* On the summit of the old city and next to its walls stands the impressive 14C–18C Gothic cathedral, dedicated to St Mary. It replaced a Romanesque cathedral of which only the bell tower and cloister now remain and is approached by no fewer than 86 steps. Don't just climb the steps for a photo opportunity and head off like many tourists do. The interior is well worth a visit.

Don't miss

♦ The **nave★★**, which is spectacularly large, and indeed is the widest in European Gothic architecture at 75ft/22.9m.

Houses along the banks of the Onyar

J. Malburet/Michelin

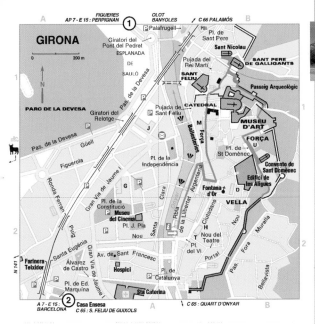

GIRONA

FIGUERES
AP 7 - E 15: PERPIGNAN
OLOT
BANYOLES
C 66 PALAMÓS

A 7 - E 15: BARCELONA
C 65: S. FELIU DE GUIXOLS
C 65: QUART D'ONYAR

- The **retable★** on the main altar (14C), the work of the Valencian silversmith Pere Bernec. It is made of gilded silver and is covered with enamels that depict scenes from Christ's life.
- **Beatus★★** A very rare 10C illuminated manuscript of the Commentary on the Apocalypse by Beatus of Liébena.
- **Tapestry of Creation★★★** A rare and large work, unique of its kind, made in the 11C or 12C. The tapestry shows iconographic details of Jewish origin adapted to the Christian religion. It depicts the creation of the world, the months of the year, and biblical characters.
- **Cloister★** Built in the 12C, it has a gallery with a double colonnade with a series of biblical scenes. It offers a welcome moment of tranquility to the

visitor and a fine view of Charlemagne's Tower.

Rambla de la Llibertat★ –
This is one of the city's busiest commercial streets. It is the main route into the old quarter, leading off the Stone Bridge, and is lined with shops and cafés. The area was a market in medieval times and bursts into color on Sunday mornings, when the flower market is held. Stroll under its ancient arches and porches and step back in time.

Sant Feliu Church★ –
Pujada de Sant Feliu. Originally a martyrium dedicated to St Felix, the current church was built on the Romanesque foundations in several stages. Of particular note are the lifesize 14C Christ and the collection of **early Christian sarcophagi★** (3C–4C).

EXCURSIONS

MONTSERRAT★★

30mi/40km from Barcelona on B23 motorway. Take the A2 motorway and leave at the Manresa exit. Take the C55 to Monistrol de Montserrat and BP1103 to Montserrat (limited parking with fees). The road to the monastery is steep and busy. You are advised to park at Cremallera Station and take the train.

Montserrat, the "jagged mountain," is one of Spain's major tourist attractions, boasting stunning scenery and a world famous monastery. It is a huge massif sculpted by wind and rain, its eroded crags resembling animals and inanimate objects. Montserrat has inspired musicians, authors, and poets, and continues to draw travelers from near and far.

Monestir de Montserrat

93 877 77 01. www.montserrat visita.com. Open daily 9am–6pm. No charge.

The monastery was founded in the 11C. It grew in importance and splendor in the 15C but was largely destroyed in 1811 during

Visiting Montserrat

The stunning and remote Benedictine monastery and its mountain is a place of pilgrimage for the Catalan people. As its website says, it is a mountain, a monastery, and a sanctuary; the website also details where to stay if you fancy spending a couple of days in the area *(www. montserratvisita.com).*

the War of Independence. Restoration began in 1844, with brief interruptions during the Spanish Civil War (1936–39), and today it is home to about 80 monks, who follow the Rule of St Benedict, devoting their lives to prayer and work, while welcoming pilgrims and visitors.

Highlights:

Basilica – *Next to the monastery. Open 7.30am–8pm.* Here you will see **La Morenata★★**, known as the "Black Virgin" (changes to the varnish have occurred over time giving the wooden figure a dark complex-

Serra de Montserrat

J. Malburet/Michelin

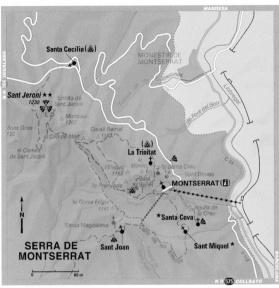

ion), a stunning 12C Romanesque polychrome carving in the upper section of the apse. Proclaimed Our Lady of Montserrat by Pope Leo XIII in 1881, the image is enthroned in a silver altarpiece *(statue on view 8am–10.30am, noon–6.30pm; www. abadiamonserrat.net).*

Gregorian chants – sung by about 50 choirboys from the Escolania de Montserrat *(Mon–Fri 1pm, Sun noon and Vespers at 6.45pm).*

Museu de Montserrat – *93 877 77 77. Open daily 10am–6.45pm. €6.50. Guided tours for groups and audio guides available.* Housed in a building designed in 1929 by Puig i Cadafalch, the museum has more than 1,300 exhibits that cover many periods, the oldest being an Egyptian sarcophagus and the most recent a sculpture from 2001 by Josep M. Subirachs. There

are wonderful works by El Greco and Caravaggio in the 13C–18C collection and in the **19C and 20C collection** are works by Picasso, Dalí, Monet, Sisley, Degas, and Pissarro. Contemporary artists feature too, with graphic works by Chagall, Braque, Miró, and Tàpies.

Panoramic views★★ – from the 15 hermitages, in particular **Sant Jeroni★★**, Montserrat's highest peak. Enjoy the breathtaking sight of the Pyrenees and Catalan coastline. Take the funicular from the monastery up to the dramatic, unspoiled peaks and follow the network of paths to the various chapels. Sant Joan is one of the most accessible. Sant Jeroni is a 90-minute walk from the funicular in the stunning Montserrat Nature Park but takes you to the highest point of the mountain at 4,055ft/1,236m.

EXCURSIONS

SITGES★★

22mi/35km southwest of Barcelona via the C32.

Sitges is one of the most popular tourist spots in Catalonia. Its long beaches attract visitors from all over the world. A town of contrasts, Sitges boasts luxury villas and modern apartments, traditional tapas bars and modern restaurants, all in a relaxed ambience.

The Old Town★★

A maze of narrow streets with whitewashed houses, flower-decorated balconies, and a variety of tempting shops and restaurants, the Old Town overlooks the breakwater of La Punta and is a perfect place to spend a few hours. You can't miss the imposing **Sant Bartomeu i Stanta Tecla church**, with its view over the long beaches offering the perfect photo opportunity. Santiago Rusiñol and Miguel Utrillo (father of the French painter) played a key role in developing the town's artistic reputation in the late 19C as can be seen in the three key museums housed in neo-Gothic mansions. It remains a popular spot for artists today.

Museu del Cau Ferrat★★ – *C. Fonollar. 93 894 03 64. www.mnac.cat/museus/sitges. Open Tue–Sat 9.30am–6.30pm, Sun 10am–3pm (closed summer 2–3.30pm and 5pm). Closed for restoration at time of going to press. €3.50.* The **Museum of Wrought Iron** is housed in the 16C home of the painter and writer Santiago Rusiñol (1861–1931) and is a temple to his philosophy of "Total Art." The exhibits include paintings, wrought-iron objects, sculptures, and ceramics, all displayed in a sumptuous setting.

Don't miss

* **Paintings** Among the works in the stunning collection in the Gothic Hall are two by El Greco (*The Tears of St Peter* and *Mary Magdalen Repentant*), brought back to Sitges from Paris by Rusiñol. There are also paintings by Picasso, Casas, Nonell, Zuloaga, and Rusiñol himself.
* **Wrought-iron pieces** These include works from many different periods and artistic styles—chandeliers, locks, keys, ornaments, and a collection of very unusual 16C door handles.

Sitges at night

J. Balanya/Michelin

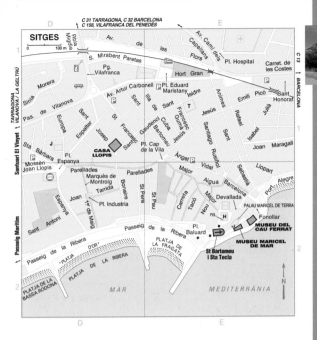

Casa Llopis★ – *Sant Gaudenci 1. 93 894 29 69. Open Tue–Sat 9.30am–6.30pm, Sun 10am–3pm (closed summer 2–3.30pm and 5pm). Combined ticket with Maricel de Mar €6.40.* Along with the Casa Papiol de Vilanova i la Geltrui, this house, built in 1793, forms the **Romantic Museum**. The various rooms with English furniture and ornate curtains bear witness to the prosperity of Sitges in the 19C. There are also clockwork models, musical boxes, and antique dolls.

Museu Maricel de Mar★ – *C. Fonollar. 93 894 03 64. Open Tue–Sat 9.30am–6.30pm, Sun 10am–3pm (closed summer 2–3.30pm and 5pm). €3.50.* This former Gothic hospital (14C), transformed in the early 20C by Miguel Utrillo, was designed to

house the collection of American billionaire, Charles Deering. The building now features Gothic mosaics, including one by San Miguel de la Torre, and displays some very varied pieces—Gothic retables, Baroque sculptures, Art Nouveau, and Renaissance furniture. There is also some excellent modern Catalan art and sculpture by Josep M. Sert.

Passeig Marítim
The Passeig Marítim runs the length of La Ribera beach and is lined with villas, hotels, shops, and restaurants. It's a great place for an early morning walk or a stroll at dusk, accompanied by joggers, dog walkers, and romantic couples.

EXCURSIONS

FIGUERES★

87mi/140km north of Barcelona on the A7 motorway.

Figueres and its most famous son, Salvador Dalí, are inextricably linked. The genius, personality, and legacy of the unique and enigmatic Surrealist artist can still be felt in the streets of the capital of the Alt Empordà district. A fascinating and dynamic tourist attraction.

Museu del Joguet★

C. de Sant Pere 1. 97 250 45 85. www. mjc.cat. Open Jun–Sept Mon–Sat 10am–7pm, Sun and public holidays 11am–6pm; Oct–May Tue–Sat 10am–6pm, Sun and public holidays 11am–2pm. Closed Jan 1, Dec 25.

The museum houses toys from all over the world and from different periods. It has a wonderful collection of automata with a particularly interesting orchestra.

Sant Ferran Castle★

Pujada del Castell. 97 251 45 85. www.castillosanfernando.org. Open daily Jul–Sept 10.30am–8pm (rest of year 10.30am–3pm).

Located to the northeast on the Pujada dell Castell and perched on a hillock, this huge fortress, one of the largest in the world, was built in the shape of a pentagon by Don Juan Martín de Cermeño from 1753 to 1766. Its purpose was to halt constant invasions from France and it provided accom-

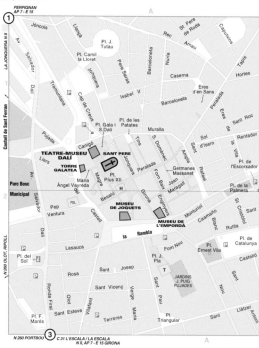

modation for 6,000 men and 500 horses. It was then turned into a military base and served as such until 1966, which explains its excellent state of preservation. If you wander around you will grasp the enormity and complexity of this type of fortification with its moat, perimeter wall, and huge water storage facility. The drinking troughs in the **stables**★ are original. Make your way to the double ring of ramparts to enjoy a fantastic **view** that stretches across the Ampurdan plain, whose fields are protected against the wind by rows of majestic cypresses. Cultural events, conventions, and trade shows are held at the castle, and its parade ground can hold up to 5,000 delegates.

© Ivan Ivanov//iStockphoto.com

Bell tower of Sant Pere Church

Torre Galatea★

Pujada del Castell.

Standing against the old Gorgot tower, this Neoclassical building was decorated by Dalí and is a foretaste of the theater and museum. He introduced ornamental motifs to the structure in his inimitable and extravagant style.

Museu de l'Empordà

Rambla 2. 97 250 23 05. www.museuemporda.org. Closed Mon. €2.

Housed in a functional modern building (1971), this museum features collections of archeology, art, and local history. It also has a large number of 19C and 20C paintings (Vayreda, Nonell, Sorolla, Dalí, Tàpies, and Joan Ponç).

Sant Pere Church

Pl. Píus XII.

This 14C church has a single aisle, both simple and stunning, and is a good example of Catalan Gothic style. The apse, transept, and recently built bell tower (1941) both complement and echo the style of the nave.

Teatre-Museu Dalí★★ *see Artists*

FIGUERES

EXCURSIONS

SPORTS AND ACTIVITIES

Barcelona is the perfect city for sporting and outdoor activities thanks to its great climate and excellent facilities and infrastructure, a legacy of the 1992 Olympic Games. It has a wide range of athletic stadiums, swimming pools, ice rinks, marinas, and even a velodrome. The locals are fanatical about football but basketball comes a close second. Here is a selection of activities and sports to either watch or take part in.

Basketball

It may come as a surprise to learn that basketball is Barcelona's second most popular spectator sport, inspiring the same fervor and celebrations for a win as for soccer. Founded in 1926, Regal FC Barcelona is a professional team that is part of FC Barcelona. One of the most successful clubs in Europe, they have played in numerous Euroleague finals and have won twice, including in 2010. Their home ground is FCB's Palau Blaugrana (M*Collblanc or Palau Reial; Travessera de les Corts 63–71; 93 902 18 99 00, www.fcbarcelona.com).*

Cycling

With a good network of cycle lanes, Barcelona is a cycle-friendly city, but if you venture out on a bike watch out for pedestrians, particularly tourists who are more likely to be admiring the scenery than paying attention to two-wheel traffic. Cycling is a good way to get around the old part of town, and you can also venture farther afield, perhaps up Montjuïc, but cyclists who are hill-averse should head for the seafront where the terrain is flatter. "Bicing" is an automated hire scheme for residents, but visitors can use rental and tour companies, which include:

Barcelona Biking – M*Jaume 1. Pl. Sant Jaume. 65 635 63 00. www. barcelonabiking.com.* Offers rental of city, road, or mountain bikes, and guided tours of the city and the immediate vicinity.

Bike Rental Barcelona – *66 605 76 55. www.bikerentalbarcelona. com.* Call to arrange pick-up, or they will deliver and collect to a specific address; guided and themed tours are available.

Cycling in front of Casa Milà

© Tupungato/Dreamstime.com

Diving with sharks

Qualified divers have the opportunity to dive with the sharks in the Oceanarium at **L'Aquàrium** *(see p 116)*. The cost covers a guided tour of the aquarium, a lecture on sharks, a dive in the Oceanarium (including use of equipment), insurance, and free entry to L'Aquàrium for two non-divers. Proof of your diving qualification is required *(see website for other requirements; Wed, Sat & Sun 9.30am–2pm. €300)*.

Golf

Thanks to the long, dry summers, Spain is a great golfing destination and has produced some excellent homegrown players (Ballesteros, García, Olazábal). If you'd like to spend time on the fairway during your stay, there are a number of attractive courses in the vicinity of Barcelona, often with superb views. You will need to book in advance, especially at weekends. Here are just a few (distances given are from the city).

Masia Bach Golf Club – *15mi/ 25km. Sant Esteve Sesrovires. 93 772 88 00. www.golfmasiabach.com/ english/promoimo.php.* Designed by José María Olazábal, a fairly challenging 18-hole course plus a more lenient 9-holes.

Pitch & Putt Badalona – *19mi/ 30km. Castillo de Godmar. 93 395 27 79. www.pitchandputt-badalona. com.* Nine holes with views over the Mediterranean, with the *castillo* in the background. Suits all levels, 18 holes + 3.

Sant Joan Golf Course – *15mi/ 25km. Rubi. 93 675 30 50. www.golf santjoan.com.* Designed by Seve Ballesteros, the only public course in Catalonia. 18 holes.

Human castles

Barcelona is famous for its *castells* or human castles, vertiginous towers built by competing teams dressed in traditional costume. It is a folk tradition that goes back several hundred years and symbolic of Catalan teamwork. The trained *castellers* stand on each other's shoulders and a child scales the final height to make the sign of the cross. The castles can be nine or ten storys high and the man atop now wears a crash helmet.

Running

Barcelona plays host to an annual marathon (Marató Barcelona) in March, when runners from all over the world come to the city. If you want to compete you must register ahead *(93 422 10 96; www.barcelona marato.es)*. Alternatives include the 7mi/11km Cursa El Corte Inglés run held in May or June *(90 112 21 22)* or the Cursa La Mercè (Barcelona Race) in September when a maximum of 10,000 runners take part in a 6mi/10km race.

Sailing

Barceloneta, the port/marina area of Barcelona, is a popular mooring for dozens of yachts, both palatial and humble. If you'd like to learn some sailing skills (or do a refresher course), there are a number of schools you can try.

Real Club Nautico de Barcelona (RCNB) – **M** *Drassanes. Moll d'Espanya. 93 221 65 21. www. escuelarcnb.com.* One of the oldest established sailing clubs in Barcelona, classes and courses cover all

SPORTS AND ACTIVITIES

The Camp Nou Experience
The "Camp Nou Experience" includes a tour of the stadium and admission to the FC Barcelona Museum. Fans can take the opportunity to run out through the tunnel onto the pitch, enjoy the view from the presidential box, explore the changing room area, and see the modern media facilities *(902 18 99 00; open daily; €17)*.

skill levels from beginner to expert, and family trips and lessons for children are also available.

Spainbookers – *www.spain bookers.com.* Pre-book online only. If you're new to sailing and want a brief taster aboard, this company runs basic two-hour starter lessons, setting out from the Centre Municipal de Vela, Port Vell. Instructors are English-speaking, and children over 7 can come along.

Costa Brava Sailing – *Port d'Aro. 97 266 24 94. www.costa-brava-sailing.com.* This company offers courses and cruises out of Port d'Aro in Palamos, near Girona. Among the options is a day's sailing down the coast to Barcelona.

⚽ Soccer: FC Barcelona

Football fans need no introduction to FC Barcelona *(www.fcbarcelona. com)*, universally known as Barça. Founded in 1899 by Swiss-born businessman Hans "Joan" Gamper, this world-famous club is the pride of the city. Sporting the UNICEF logo on its strip and devoting 0.7 percent of revenue to international development, Barça is "more than a club," it is also an ambassador for Catalonia. With supporter clubs all over the world, Barça is owned by its 170,000 socis (members), who elect the president. Many great players have pulled on the famous claret and blue strip, including Maradona, Guardiola, Ronaldo, Figo, Ronaldinho, and Messi. Over a long history Barça have won countless honors, including 20 Spanish League titles, three Champions Leagues and one FIFA Club World Cup.

Past managers include Frank Rijkaard, Bobby Robson, and Johan Cruyff, architect of the famous Dream Team, which won the Spanish League four years running, as well as the club's first ever European Cup (now the Champions League).

Camp Nou – Ⓜ *Les Corts, Collblanc. Av. Arístides Maillol. 93 902 18 99 00. www.fcbarcelona.com.* The home of FC Barçelona, Camp Nou stadium is easily accessible by bus, metro or tram. The impressive 99,000-capacity stadium—soon to be remodeled and expanded to Sir Norman Foster's futuristic design—has also served as the venue for World Cup matches, Cup Winners' Cup, and Champions League finals and the final of the 1992 Olympic Games football championship. It is also used for special events and pop concerts.

FC Barcelona Museum – Recently modernized, this is the city's most popular museum. The exhibits range from Kubala's boots and the shirt worn by Johan Cruyff in the 5-0 away thrashing of eternal rivals Real Madrid to a display of all the club's many trophies. There is also a multimedia zone, including screens showing great goals in the club's history. The shop sells a full range of Barça souvenirs and products.

Sunbathing

The longest and busiest beaches can be found at Sant Sebastià and Barceloneta, which are also the most central. Farther east, Nova Icària and Bogatell beaches are almost as long but a little quieter. Beyond that again is Mar Bella beach, which includes a partially screened naturist beach. The farthest and quietest beaches are Nova Mar Bella and Llevant, both accessed from the metro at Selva de Mar.

Swimming

If you prefer a pool to the beach, Barcelona has some great choices over and above the usual health-club-style pool. Try the Olympic pool up on Montjuïc, or take a picnic to the lake in the Parc de la Creueta dell Coll. Alternatively, if you want a family outing and have your own transport, try one of the many water adventure parks that dot the country around Barcelona.

Piscinas Picornell – ⓂEspanya. Av. de l'Estadi 30–40. 93 423 40 41. www.picornell.com. Indoor pool: Open Mon–Fri 6.45am–noon, Sat 7am–9pm, Sun 7.30am–4pm (Jun–Sept 8pm). Outdoor pool: Open daily Jun–Sept 9am–9pm (Sun 8pm); Mar–May & Oct–Nov 10am–6pm (Sun 4pm); Dec–Feb 10am–4.30pm (Sun 4pm). Revamped in 1992 for the Olympics, this swimming complex has two pools, one heated, indoors, and one outside with the most stunning views of the city laid out below Montjuïc.

Parc de la Creueta del Coll – ⓂVallcarca. Pg Mare de Déu del Coll 77. 93 424 38 09. www.bcn.cat/parcsijardins. Open daily 1 Jun–31 Aug 10am–4pm (Sat–Sun 8pm). This pretty park has been made in a disused quarry near to Parc Güell. Its centerpiece is a lake with a little palm-planted island which in summer becomes a swimming pool.

Costa Caribe – 60mi/96km south of Barcelona. Port Aventura, Tarragona. www.portaventura.es. An aquatic adventure park near the resort of Tarragona, this makes for a good family day out. It's usually open between March and December, but check before you go, as opening hours vary and you'll be able to get cheaper tickets in advance online.

Camp Nou, FC Barcelona

©FC Barcelona

FOR KIDS

Kids can soon get tired and restless when visiting a big city, especially when the sun's shining. However, Barcelona has plenty of kid-friendly attractions, including fun activities at the museums, an aquarium, and a zoo, as well as some great green spaces where they can let off steam. And of course, there's always the beach... For more information on activities for kids, check out www.kidsinbarcelona.com.

Fundació Joan Miró★★★ –

see p 84. Joan Miró's bright, bold colors and his unconventional, almost childlike artistic style tend to appeal to kids of any age, so a visit here will capture their interest and imagination. Between October and May, the foundation stages shows for children that, although performed in Catalan, are highly entertaining *(Oct–May Sat 5.30pm, Sun and public holidays 11.30am and 1pm; €4).*

L'Aquàrium★

Ⓜ *Drassanes (L3), Barceloneta (L4). Moll d'Espanya del Port Vell. 93 221 74 74. www.aquarium.bcn. com. Open Mon–Fri 9.30am–9pm (Jun & Sept 9.30pm, Jul & Aug 11pm) Sat, Sun, public holidays 9.30am–9.30pm. €17.50.*

This is one of the finest aquariums in Europe, and its mission is to make learning "fun and a delight." Here you can trace the develop-

ment of all kinds of specimens in the Mediterranean and tropical tanks—about 450 different species in all. Under the wary eyes of the sharks, you can walk through the **Oceanarium** via a transparent 262ft/80m tunnel that gives you the impression of walking on the sea bed. **Planeta Aqua** reveals how sea creatures have adapted to diverse conditions in their environment, while **Miniacuaria** takes a look at the less conspicuous flora and fauna. A particular highlight is the L'Aquàrium's fascinating collection of mollusk shells. A fun place to spend time and educational too, **Explora!** allows youngsters to take part in interactive activities.

Museu d'Arqueològia de Catalunya★ – *see p 79.* Between October and May, Sunday is designated children's day at the museum, with a different activity planned every week. The first Sunday of the month is aimed at 3–5-year-olds

L'Aquàrium

©Turespaña

Female giant anteater, Zoo Barcelona

Jordi Fabregas/Zoo Barcelona

while the remaining Sundays are for 6–12-year-olds. The workshops are a great introduction to various periods of Spanish history through role play, puzzles and quizzes, rock painting, and even some hands-on archeology.

Museu de Ciències Naturals★

www.bcn.cat/museuciencies. The museum is currently closed for reorganization.

The Natural Sciences Museum, which comprises the former Museu de Zoologia and Museu de Geologia, is currently being reorganized and when complete *(scheduled for early 2011)* will be housed in the **Espai Blau** (the Forum building, built for the 2004 Universal Forum of Cultures). As well as the new permanent exhibition, entitled Planet Life, there will be temporary exhibitions and a range of educational activities.

Museu Frederic Marès★ – see p 89. – see p 89. Children of all ages will be fascinated by the contents of the **Cabinet of Curiosities** and enchanted by the collection of antique toys.

Museu Marítim★ – see p 80.
The full-size model of a galleon is a great attraction for kids, and if they really want to get a feel for life in the galleys in the 16C, then "Galiots!" will do just that—this activity takes place on the third Saturday of every month and adults can join in too *(advance booking required)*.

Poble Espanyol★ – see p 52.
A treasure hunt is a great way for families to discover Poble Espanyol in Montjuïc—you buy a game pack *(€5 for a family of up to five members; children aged 9 and under must be accompanied)*, which comprises a backpack with materials with all the clues to help you unearth the secrets of the fascinating reproduction Spanish village.

Zoo Barcelona★

Ⓜ *Marina, Arc de Triomf (L1), Barceloneta, Ciutadella/Vila Olímpica (L4). Parc de la Ciutadella. 93 225 67 80. www.zoobarcelona.com. Open daily Nov–Mar 10am–5.30pm (last entry 5pm), Apr–mid-May, Oct 10am–7pm (last entry 6pm), mid-May–mid-Sept 10am–8pm (last admission 7pm). Dec 25 10am–noon. €16.*

117

Although it has lost its star attraction, Flocon de Neige (Snowflake, a rare albino gorilla, who died in 2003), the zoo has a wide selection of animals on display (more than 4,000, representing 400 different species) including dolphins, which put on a show twice daily. Children aged 4–11 can learn about how the dolphins are trained, and much more besides, during one of the "Mornings at the Zoo" sessions *(Sat 10am–1pm)*. While you're wandering around the zoo, look out for the famous *Woman with Umbrella*, a sculpture of a young woman dressed in period costume (1884).

Bubbleparc

Ⓜ *Drassanes (L3). Pl. de l'Odissea, Maremagnum shopping mall, Port Vell. www.maremagnum.es. Open daily Jun–Sept 11am–9pm. Rides individually priced.*

When the kids need to let off a little steam, Bubbleparc is a great place to go, even with very young children. There's a Bungydome with a reverse bungy jump (you go up rather than down), a Triketrack circuit, Acuaboats, and the Bubblepool, where you walk

on water inside a giant transparent bubblepod—more of a challenge than it sounds!

CaixaForum – *see p 80.* Family activities on offer at the city's cultural and educational center include children's cinema and theater and interactive exhibits. Children can also take part in workshops.

CosmoCaixa – Museu de la Ciència

Ⓜ *Av. del Tibidabo (L7, L3). At the foot of Tibidabo. Isaac Newton 26. 93 212 60 50. www.cosmocaixa.com. Open Tue–Sun 10am–8pm. Closed Jan 1 & 6, Dec 25. €3 (free the first Sun of the month; activities not included in admission price).*

Barcelona's new science museum opened in 2005 and is said to be one of the best in Europe. Ideal to visit with even the youngest of children, it combines scientific knowledge with entertainment. Here you'll find a Foucault pendulum, a reproduction of the Amazon rainforest—complete with alligators, snakes, and birds, a planetarium, and a geological wall. There are also workshops where

Triketrack circuit, Bubbleparc

Alan Moore/Michelin

you can conduct experiments that are both fascinating and fun, as well as a whole range of activities including treasure hunts.

El Rei de la Màgia

Ⓜ *Jaume 1 (L4). C. de L'Oli 6. 93 319 39 20. Open Sept–Jul Sat 6pm, Sun noon. €7. Admission includes children's magic show.*

The museum of magic opens only at show times and a combined ticket gives entrance to the museum and a children's magic show. There is also a shop nearby *(C. de la Princesa 11, www.elreydelamagia. com)*, established in 1881 to sell the necessary equipment for performing magic tricks.

Museu de Cera

Ⓜ *Drassanes (L3). Pg de la Banca 7. 93 317 26 49 www.museocera bcn.com. Open daily Jul–Aug 10am–10pm; rest of year Mon–Fri 10.30am–1.30pm, 4–7.30pm, Sat, Sun 11am–2pm, 4.30–8.30pm. €12.*

Barcelona's wax museum is housed in a charming 19C mansion. Ancient sculptures sit alongside Superman and the famous *Star Wars* android, C-3PO—in total there are more than 300 figures representing famous characters, both real and fictional, from various periods. The museum's "fairy forest" café, El Bosc de les Fades, is worth a visit.

🍫 **Museu de la Xocolata** – *see p 41.* Not only is the musuem a great place to visit with young chocolaholics or budding chocolatiers, but they can also join in workshops catering to dif-

©Sara Fernandez Garcia/El Rei de la Màgia

El Rei de la Màgia

ferent age groups *(see website for details—advance booking required)*. Children aged 3–12 can even have their birthday parties here—the package includes a tour of the museum, a workshop, and a taste of the chocolate goodies.

Seaside—Barcelona beaches

– The beaches around Barcelona are really geared up for kids, even to the extent of offering a lending service for necessities such as buckets and spades, petanque sets, etc, as well as running kite-flying courses and boat trips *(Centre de la Platja, near Hospital del Mar, Barceloneta beach; Jul–Sept)*. For bookworms, libraries keep a selection of children's books and comics in a variety of languages *(Espigó de Bac de Roda on Mar Bella beach and Centre de la Platja, see above)*. There are also many children's play areas *(Sant Sebastià/Barceloneta beach and Mar Bella beach)*. At Parc Forum, an area of the sea is sectioned off between May and October to create a safe, shallow, natural swimming pool.

NIGHTLIFE

The city nightlife is varied, lively, and often noisy. Bars, clubs, and music venues abound, and cinemas are plentiful too, with some screening films in English. Many theaters and concert halls have more than one auditorium enabling them to stage a range of performing arts. Whatever your preference, you will find something to entertain you in Barcelona.

Theater, music, and dance

There are many theater and concert venues in Barcelona. A number are housed in beautiful old buildings that have been given a new lease of life, or in new, purpose-built ones at the cutting edge of design.

🚇 Palau de la Música Catalana★★

Ⓜ *Urquinaona. C. Palau de la Música 4. 93 295 72 00. www.palaumusica.org.*

A fabulous example of the Modernista style, the building has been designated a UNESCO World Heritage Site. A modern extension contains another hall and a restaurant. The program ranges from classical and jazz to Brazilian, fado, and Catalan. Ella Fitzgerald and Rachmaninov have both performed here.

Gran Teatre del Liceu★

Ⓜ *Liceu. La Rambla 51–59. 93 485 99 00. www.liceubarcelona.com.*

Opened in 1847, the building has had a checkered history. Devastated by fire in 1861 and again in 1994, it was targeted by anarchists in 1893. One of the largest venues of its kind in Europe, the Liceu has premiered the work of Richard Wagner, hosted ballets by Diaghilev, and staged performances by great singers such as Montserrat Caballé. The program features classic opera and dance.

Teatre Grec★

Ⓜ *Poble Sec. Funicular at Paral.lel. Montjuïc. 93 316 10 00. www.barcelonafestival.com.*

This outdoor Greek-style amphitheater, was built for the 1929 International Exhibition. In

Gran Teatre del Liceu

©Turespaña

summer it stages performances during the city's Festival del Grec.

L'Auditori

🅼 *Marina. C. Lepant 150, Poble Nou. 93 326 29 45. www.auditori.com.*

Opened in 1999, the three halls—named after Catalan musicians Pau Casals, Oriol Martorell, and Tete Montoliu—have made it a top venue for musical performances of all kinds. It is the home of the Orquestra Simfònica de Barcelona and the Museu de la Música *(Museum of Music; 93 256 36 50; www.museumusica.bcn.cat; open Mon–Sat 10am–6pm, Sun 8pm).*

Tablao de Carmen

🅼 *Espanya. Av. de Comillas, Monjuïc. 93 325 68 95. www.tablaodecarmen.com.*

In the Poble Espanyol *(see p 52).* This venue was established in 1988 as a tribute to the dancer Carmen Amaya, who was born in a Barcelona slum and went on to perform at the White House. The entrance charge includes dinner, drinks, or tapas, with two shows a night.

 Tablao Flamenco Cordobés

🅼 *Liceu. La Rambla 35. 93 317 57 11. www.tablaocordobes.com/.*

All the great artists have performed at this famous venue. Shows last approximately 1hr 15min.

Teatre Lliure

🅼 *Poble Sec. Pl. Margarida Xirgu 1. Pg de Santa Madrona 40-46. 93 228 97 47. www.teatrelliure.com.*

Sardana

Sardana is a powerful symbol of Catalan cultural identity. Forming a small circle, hands joined and raised, the dancers perform neat, precise steps. The circle grows as more people join in—and if the original becomes too large, a new one is formed. It is performed regularly, including in front of the cathedral and/or Pl. St Jaume Saturday/Sunday evening, and plays a major part in Barcelona's many festivals.

©Turespaña
Sardana dancing

The complex comprises the Lliure de Gràcia *(closed for restoration at the time of going to press),* Sala Fabià Puigserver, and Espai Lliure, a more intimate venue. They stage a range of theater, dance, and musical performances, some with English subtitles *(Thu and Sat nights).*

Teatre Mercat de les Flors

🅼 *Poble Sec. C. Lleida 59. 93 426 18 75. www.mercatflors.org.*

On the site of a former flower market, this theater specializes in contemporary dance featuring both international and home-grown performers and includes some experimental productions.

Teatre Nacional de Catalunya

Ⓜ *Glòries. Pl. de les Arts 1. 93 306 57 00. www.tnc.cat.*

The National Theater of Catalonia is in an impressive modern building designed by Ricardo Bofill. A vast glass lobby welcomes theater-goers as they make their way to one of the three performance areas. The program (drama, dance, music) is mainly in Catalan.

Cinemas

Most of the city's cinemas show commercial movies dubbed into Spanish. However, some screen movies in "VO" (versión original), which more often than not will be English.

Cinema Maldà

Ⓜ *Liceu. C. del Pi 5. 93 481 37 04. cinemamalda.net/.*

Maldà screens indie and arthouse movies and documentaries from around the world.

Méliès

Ⓜ *Urgell. C. Villarroel 102. 93 451 00 55. www.cinesmelies.net.*

A mix of arthouse and classic movies on two screens, with retrospectives and theme weeks.

Verdi & Verdi Park

Ⓜ *Fontana. C. Verdi 32. C. Torrijos 49. 93 238 79 90. www.cines-verdi.com.*

Two cinemas for movie buffs, around the corner from each other. They have nine screens between them, devoted largely to indie movies.

Yelmo Icaria

Ⓜ *Ciutadella/Vila Olímpica. C. Salvador Espriú 61. 93 221 75 85. www.yelmocineplex.es/.*

In a shopping mall in the Olympic Village, 15 screens show all the latest commercial movies.

Live music

You can listen to all kinds of live music in the city, at venues ranging from intimate clubs to vast halls. Here is just a small selection.

Bikini

Ⓜ *Entença. C. Déu i Mata 105. 93 322 08 00. www.bikinibcn.com.*

Sala Bikini, has long been a benchmark in Barcelona nightlife, as well as a launch pad for local artists. Nightly DJ sessions and regular concerts with artists from Bettye Lavette to Youssou N'Dour.

Harlem Jazz Club

Ⓜ *Jaume 1. C. de la Comtessa de Sobradiel 8. 93 310 07 55. www.harlemjazzclub.es.*

A classic Barcelona venue. Live shows nightly at 10.30pm and midnight (1hr later on Fri and Sat). Featuring a varied menu of jazz, funk, blues, Brazilian, and Cuban sounds, and much more.

Jamboree

Ⓜ *Liceu. Pl. Reial 17. 93 319 17 89. www.masimas.com/jamboree.*

A live music club specializing in jazz in all its variants—Latin, World, blues. Performances nightly. Head upstairs to Los Tarantos for more traditional flamenco shows.

©Greg Gladman/APA Publications

Harlem Jazz Club

Luz de Gas

Ⓜ *Muntaner. C. Muntaner 246. 93 209 77 11. www.luzdegas.com.*

One of the most attractive and unusual live music venues in the city. It hosts an impressive monthly program of live concerts featuring a wide range of musical styles.

Razzmatazz

Ⓜ *Bogatell. C. de Pamplona 88, 1er piso. 93 320 82 00. www.salarazzmatazz.com.*

Razzmatazz houses three multi-purpose rooms in the Poble Nou district, staging live music, exhibitions, parties, and fashion shows. The rooms include the largest concert hall of its type in Barcelona, holding up to 3,000 people.

Sala Apolo

Ⓜ *Para.lel. C. Nou de la Rambla 111. 93 441 40 01. www.sala-apolo.com.*

An outstanding live music venue that's been open since before the Civil War. Originally a ballroom, it was converted into a concert hall and nightclub in 1991 and

a second venue was opened in 2006. Rock, pop, fusion, world, jazz, swing, flamenco, you name it…

Bars

Bar Boadas

Ⓜ *Catalunya. C. Tallers 1. 93 318 95 92. Open Mon–Sat noon–2am.*

Not just one of the best cocktail bars in Barcelona, one of the best in the world! The founder learned his trade at Hemingway's Floridita Bar in Havana. Try the daiquiris, or the excellent martinis, and check out the art of past patrons, including Joan Miró, on the walls.

Bar del Pi

Ⓜ *Liceu. Pl. de Sant Josep Oriol 1. 93 302 21 23. www.bardelpi.com. Open Mon–Fri 9am–11pm, Sat 9.30am–10.30pm, Sun 10am–10pm.*

The Unified Socialist Party of Catalonia was founded here, but you don't need to be political to enjoy the boho atmosphere. There's a shady terrace on which to enjoy coffee, pastries, wine, and tapas.

Bar Boadas

©Gregory Wrona/APA Publications

NIGHTLIFE

Bar Virreina

🅜 *Fontana. Pl. de la Virreina 1. 93 237 98 80. Open daily noon–2am.*

Gràcia's most coveted terrace for a rendezvous over a morning coffee, an afternoon beer, or a vermouth sundowner.

Bodega Raim

🅜 *Fontana. C. Progrés 48. www.raimbcn.com. Open daily 8pm–2.30am.*

A typical little bodega with owners who clearly love everything Cuban. Popular among Gràcia trendies for its mojitos.

Can Paixano

🅜 *Barceloneta. C. Reina Cristina 7. 93 310 08 39. www.canpaixano.com. Open Mon–Sat 9am–10.30pm.*

Better known as Xampanyería, this bar is a classic destination to get the evening going. Regulars and students mingle under the swinging hams, and the cheap-and-cheerful cava flows.

Casa Almirall

🅜 *Universitat. C. Joaquín Costa 33. 93 318 99 17. Open daily 7pm–3am.*

Rather dark inside, but full of character, with its marble tables and bar, and faded Art Nouveau charm (founded 1860). Comfy seating, good music, great atmosphere.

Gimlet

🅜 *Jaume 1. C. del Rec 24. 93 310 10 27. Open daily 8pm–3am.*

If you're a cocktail lover, look no farther. A small retro bar to which a local clientele has been gravitating since forever and a day.

🐾 La Caseta del Migdia

🅜 *Paral.lel. Funicular Montjuïc. Mirador del Migdia. 61 795 65 72. www.lacaseta.org. Open Jun–Sept Wed 8pm–midnight (Thu 1am, Fri 2am), Sat noon–2am (Sun 1am).*

From the terrace of this charming little house, you'll find one of the best vantage points in Barcelona from which to watch the sunset, and DJs providing the sounds.

La Vinya del Senyor

R. Mattes/Michelin

La Vinya del Senyor

🅼 *Jaume 1. Pl. Santa Maria 5. 93 310 33 79. Open Mon–Thu noon–1am, Fri–Sat noon–2am, Sun noon–midnight.*

A bar with two floors and a large terrace at the foot of Santa Maria del Mar church. Bliss for a bite to eat or an aperitif in the evening.

Clubs

Club Fellini

🅼 *Liceu. La Rambla 27. 93 272 49 80. www.clubfellini.com. Open Mon, Thu–Sat from 12pm.*

Three dance floors pulsate to sessions by resident and guest DJs, playing electro, house, and techno.

Macarena Club

🅼 *Drassanes. C. Nou de Sant Francesc 5. 93 317 54 36. www.macarenaclub.com. Open Thu–Sun from midnight.*

Housed in a former flamenco club, this tiny venue serves up a big sound and a wide range of music.

Magic Club

🅼 *Barceloneta. Pg Picasso 40. 93 310 72 67. www.magic-club.net. Open Thu–Sun from midnight.*

Serving up hard rock since the 70s, Magic takes you for a walk on the wild side. The posters of the Ramones and Elvis give you a clue to what awaits.

Moog

🅼 *Drassanes. C. Arc del Teatre 3. 93 301 72 82. www.masimas.com/moog. Open daily from midnight.*

A romantic evening
Begin in the café at the top of **El Corte Inglés** *(see p 126)*, from where you can enjoy the breathtaking view across the city at dusk. Stroll down the Rambla and duck into the **Plaça Reial** for a cocktail. Enjoy local delicacies in one of the many tapas bars along Carrer Ample or Carrer de la Mercè and then choose between a night of dancing at a club or a walk along the beach. Barcelona perfection!

One of the smallest clubs in the city, popular with members of the local underground scene. Central dance floor with a smaller chillout room upstairs.

Otto Zutz

🅼 *Fontana. C. Lincoln 15. 93 238 07 22. www.grupo-ottozutz.com/. Open Wed–Sat from noon.*

Eternal, smart, elegant, the place to see and be seen. A veteran of the scene with VIP space where you can look down on the rest as they dance to the best funk, hip-hop, and house. Local celebrities often drop in.

Sidecar Factory Club

🅼 *Liceu. Pl. Reial 7. 93 302 15 86. www.sidecarfactoryclub.com. Open Mon–Thu 6pm–4.30am (Fri, Sat 5am).*

A club that has launched the careers of many acts such as Manu Chao and Sisa, and remains faithful to its commitment to live music and to local groups.

NIGHTLIFE

SHOPPING

It may not have a reputation as one of the great shopping meccas, but Barcelona offers a variety and a quirkiness that are not easily matched elsewhere—a vibrant mix of small independent, specialist stores, many of which have been trading for decades, if not centuries, and a good selection of interesting department stores and high street chains. Shopping is fairly well dispersed across the city, so whichever district you find yourself in there's sure to be somewhere interesting to browse. Be aware of *la tarde*—the shopping siesta that applies to the majority of more traditional shops; many stores close at lunchtime and don't reopen until around 4pm. To compensate, most stay open until around 8pm, but check out individual opening hours if you have a specific shop in mind.

MAINSTREAM SHOPPING

If you like the buzz offered by malls and department stores, or are looking for the best of Camper or Zara, here is some of the best of Barcelona's mainstream shopping.

Department stores and malls

El Corte Inglés

🅜 *Catalunya. Pl. de Catalunya 14. 93 306 38 00. www.elcorteingles. es. Open 10am–10pm.*

The grande dame of Barcelona's shops, this monolithic department store sells everything from lint rollers and expensive chocolates to clothes and furniture. It's justly seen as a Barcelona institution, and while its interior may be a little careworn in places it's worth a visit if only for its great air conditioning.

L'illa Diagonal

🅜 *Maria Cristina. Av. Diagonal 545. 93 444 00 00. www.lilla.com. Open 10am–9.30pm.*

Designed by star architects Rafael Moneo and Ignasi de Sola-Moralies, this mall combines a wealth of bookstores, clothes shops, accessory and gift outlets, as well as a hotel and various places to eat.

Maremagnum

🅜 *Drassanes. Moll d'Espanya 5. 93 225 81 00. www.maremagnum.es. Open Mon–Sun 10am–10pm (bars open 11pm–4.30am).*

From a distance this huge mall, built as part of Barcelona's port regeneration project, is designed to look like a ship in full sail. Inside, it caters for both shoppers and fun-seekers, with a huge selection of shops and concessions of every kind, whether you're hunting for designer labels, novelty objects, a showing of the latest movie, or something to eat.

Maremagnum

Alan Moore/Michelin

MUST DO

Chainstores

Camper

Ⓜ *Liceu. C. Elisabets 11. 93 342 41 41. www.camper.com. Open Mon–Sat 9.30am–1.30pm, 4.30–8pm.*

Camper have established themselves as a lifestyle brand as well as an internationally popular manufacturer of shoes—and this store sits alongside Casa Camper, one of the chain's new hotels. There's a good range of footwear in the shop; the hotel is small, eco in its approach, and very popular.

Desigual

Ⓜ *Jaume 1, Urquinaona. C. Arcs 9. 93 215 08 84. www.desigual.com. Open Mon–Sat 10am–10pm.*

The concept store of the popular design chain has an impressive interior—all the better to showcase the clothes that its followers admire. High-end fashion at mid-market prices make this a destination shop.

Mango

Ⓜ *Pl. de Gracia. Pl. de Gracia 65. 93 215 75 30. www.mango.com. Open Mon–Sat 10am–8.30pm.*

Alan Moore/Michelin
Camper store

Zara's little sister is a fantastic find for younger fashionistas, and this store is one of the best-stocked in the chain. Packed with young and hip clothes, it's a great place to update your look at very competitive prices.

Zara

Ⓜ *Pl. de Gracia. Pl. de Gracia 16. 93 318 76 76. www.zara.com. Open Mon–Fri 9.30am–2pm, 4–7.30pm, Sat 10am–2pm.*

If you feel too grown up for some of Mango's offerings, just walk up Gracia to find the Zara store. Cheap, stylish, and with ever-changing stock, you're sure to find something here to suit, and this branch also incorporates a Zara Home.

SHOPPING

SPECIALIST SHOPS

Away from the big designer names, the malls, and the department stores, Barcelona is home to dozens of smaller shops, many of which are very individual in character. Here are some firmly established favorites.

Clothes and shoes

Custo Barcelona

Ⓜ *Jaume 1. Pl. de les Olles 7. 93 268 78 93. www.custo-barcelona. com. Open Mon–Sat 10am– 9.30pm.*

Home to the colorful confections of Custo Dalmau, Catalonia's famous home-grown designer. The Custo look, with its bright prints and playful proportions, is showstopping.

Erase una vez

Ⓜ *Diagonal. C. Goya 7. 93 217 29 77. www.eraseunavez.info. Open Mon 5–9pm, Tue–Sat 11am– 2pm, 5.30–9pm.*

A little boutique in the heart of Gracia selling the creations of young designers. With its floaty fabrics and pretty styles, this boutique is a great showcase of Catalan design.

Holala! Plaza

Ⓜ *Universitat. Pl. de Castella 2. 93 302 05 93. www.holala-ibiza.com. Open Mon–Sat 11am–9pm.*

Barcelona's latest mecca for vintage clothes, a boutique specializing in secondhand finery for the young and on-trend. It also has a range of gloriously kitsch accessories.

Jean Pierre Bua

Ⓜ *Diagonal. Av. Diagonal 467–9. 934 444 962. www.jeanpierre bua. com. Open Mon–Sat 10am–2pm, 4.30–8.30pm.*

A high-fashion store with a particularly diverse stock by both Spanish and international designers. Pricey, but the beautiful clothes are well worth their price tags.

Magatzems del Pilar

Ⓜ *Liceu. C. de la Boqueria 43. 93 317 79 84. www.almacenes-delpilar.com. Open Mon–Sat 9.30am–2pm, 4–8pm.*

With a seductive array of traditional flamenco dresses (sevillanas), shoes, fans, and shawls, this shop is a must if you want to channel true flamenco style.

La Manual Alpargatera

Ⓜ *Jaume 1. C. d'Avinyó 7. 93 301 01 72. www.lamanualpargatera.com. Open Mon–Sat 9.30am–1.30pm, 4.30–8pm. Closed Oct–Nov.*

An annual summer stop for most natives of Barcelona, this shop sells authentic Catalan rope-soled espadrilles. If that sounds limited, think again: these fabulously comfortable shoes are available in a lavish array of styles and colors.

Muxart

Ⓜ *Diagonal. C. del Rosello 230. 93 488 10 64. www.muxart.com. Open Mon–Sat, 9.30am–1.30pm, 4.30–8pm.*

If designer shoes are your bag, this is the ultimate stop-off in the city. Muxart shoes are unique: beautifully made with odd, offbeat shapes and wonderful textures and colors. These little works of art come at a price, but if you're a shoe enthusiast, you won't hesitate. Plus, the shop has an equally desirable range of bags and belts to match.

Sombreria Obach

Ⓜ *Jaume 1, Liceu. C. del Call 2. 93 318 40 94. Open Mon–Fri 9.30am–1.30pm, 4–8pm, Sat 9.30am–1.45pm, 4.30–8pm.*

Sombreria Obach

Alan Moore/Michelin

Stock varies from the traditional (such as the barret, the characteristic red Catalan hat, and beautiful black felt sombreros) to the more everyday—straw hats, fedoras, and berets. Helpful staff and a lovely old-fashioned atmosphere make this a relaxed place to spend a while trying all the different styles.

Bookshops

Boutique de la Fundació Joan Miró

Funicular de Montjuïc. Parc de Montjuïc. 93 443 94 96. www. fundacio-miro-bcn.org. Open Tue–Sat 10am–7pm (Jul–Sept 9pm), Sun 10am–2.30pm.

The book and gift shop of the Miró foundation offers not only a wide range of merchandise inspired by the brilliant Catalan artist, but also the latest in cute and contemporary design objects. In the bookstore, there's a huge selection of works on art, architecture, and design.

La Central del Macba

Ⓜ *Liceu. Pl. dels Àngels. 93 412 59 08. www.lacentral.com. Open Sept 25–Jun 24 Mon–Fri 10am–8pm (Sat 8.30pm, Sun 3pm); Jun 25–Sept 24 Mon–Fri 10.30am–8.30pm (Sat 10am–8.30pm, Sun 10am–3pm).*

La Central del Raval

Ⓜ *Catalunya. C. Elisabets 6. 90 288 49 90. www.lacentral.com. Open Mon–Fri 9.30am–9pm, Sat 10am–9pm.*

The Central shops have the best selection of contemporary arts books and DVDs in Barcelona, plus a handful of designer products. They're great spots for browsing and stay open through the middle of the day, so you can wile away a peaceful hour or two while most other stores are closed. The Raval shop is located within the walls of the late 17C church of Nostra Signora della Misericordia, and the national and international press is available in its café-restaurant.

Alan Moore/Michelin
La Central del Raval

Design, gifts, and interiors

L'appartement

🅼 *Diagonal. C. d'Enric Granados 44. 93 452 29 04. www.lapparte ment.es. Open Tue–Sat 10.30am– 2.30pm, 4.30–8.30pm.*

An Aladdin's cave of a concept store, part gallery, part cool boutique, where you'll find eclectic design objects to suit all budgets. Well worth exploring.

⚜ Cereria Subirà

🅼 *Jaume 1. Baixada de la Llibretaria 7. 93 315 26 06. Open Mon–Fri 9am–1.30pm, 4–7.30pm, Sat 9am–1.30pm.*

Dating from 1761, this is the oldest shop in Barcelona, specializing in the manufacture and sale of every possible kind and color of candle. The decorative interior dates from the 19C. Charming service.

Papirum

🅼 *Jaume 1. Baixada de la Llibreteria 2. 93 310 52 42. Open Mon–Fri 10am–8.30pm, Sat 10am–2pm, 5–8.30pm.*

This tiny shop is crammed with pens, stationery, handmade writing paper, and anything else you can imagine to do with writing. It's a bit small for sustained browsing, but you're likely to find something desirable within minutes.

Ultima Parada

🅼 *Poblenou. C. Taulat 93. 93 221 80 78. www.ultima-parada. com. Open Mon–Sat 10am–2pm, 4–7.30pm.*

Alan Moore/Michelin

Antiquing in Barcelona

If you want to look for antiques and curiosities in locations other than Barcelona's flea markets, head for the Barri Gòtic and take a stroll along the C. del Banys Nous and the C. de la Palla—both have a selection of smaller shops with interesting stock. In the Eixample district, head for Pl. de Gracia 55 where, in the Bulevard Rosa shopping center, you'll find the Bulevard dels Antiquari, with more than 70 dealers in all sorts of curios.

An invaluable address for sourcing industrial furnishings, lamps, and offbeat objects of all eras. Advertising and film stylists are regular customers, which figures, as it's a treasure trove of the unusual.

⚜ Vinçon

🅼 *Diagonal. Pg de Gracia 96. 93 215 60 50. Open Mon–Sat 10am– 8.30pm.*

This veritable temple of design extends over two floors and offers everything from kitchen utensils to contemporary furniture. There's an unusual view of Gaudís La Pedrera (Casa Milà) from the first floor.

MUST DO

FOOD AND DRINK

If you fancy a picnic, there are plenty of great shops where you can pick up all you need, plus a few luxuries to take back home.

Delicatessens

Casa Guinart

Ⓜ *Liceu. La Rambla 95. 93 317 88 87. www.casaguinart.com. Open Mon–Sat 9am–9pm.*

Located beside the exit of the Boqueria market, this purveyor of fine food is over 100 years old. You'll find ham, cheese, and wine, all carefully selected and of supreme quality—great for immediate consumption or to take home.

Colmado Quilez

Ⓜ *Pl. de Gracia. Rambla de Catalunya 63. 93 215 87 85. www.la fuente.es. Open Mon–Sat 9am–2pm, 4.30–8.30pm, Sun 9am–2pm.*

A vast, century-old *colmado* (traditional grocery store) where you'll find foie gras, caviar, manchego cheese, fuets (salami), sobresada (spicy sausage), preserves, wine, and many liqueurs all arrayed in a fantastic display.

Cakes and chocolate

Chocolateria Valor

Ⓜ *Jaume 1. C. Tapineria 10. 93 487 62 46. www.valor.es. Open Mon–Fri 8.30am–12.30pm, 4.30–11pm, Sat–Sun 9am–1pm.*

Try the hot chocolate with interesting additions in this little café—one of a popular Spanish chain—or order up a takeaway of one of their cocoa-infused specialties.

Foix de Sarrià

Ⓜ *Reina Elisenda. C. Major de Sarrià 57. 93 203 07 14. www.foixdesarria.com. Open Mon–Sun 8am–9pm.*

Foodies will have a field day at this renowned cake shop which specializes in Catalan confectionery. It's a little out of the way, but a cup of coffee and a pastry will set you up for exploring the Sarrià area of upper Barcelona, which still has a villagey feel.

Xocoa

Ⓜ *Jaume 1. C. Vidreria 4. 93 553 99 34. www.xocoa-bcn.com. Open Mon–Sun 9am–9pm.*

You can follow your nose to the door of this chocolate shop from several streets away. The success of Xocoa is down to astute design as well as high-quality chocolate.

Wine and cava

El Celler de la Boqueria

Ⓜ *Liceu. C. de la Petxina 9. 90 288 92 63. www.cellerboqueria.com. Open Tue–Sun 9.30am–2.30pm, 5–8pm.*

A large selection of cavas and Catalan and Spanish wines, well priced and classified by region.

Xampany

Ⓜ *Universitat. C. de Valencia 200. 67 084 50 11. Open Mon–Fri 10am–1.30pm, 4.30–8pm, Sat 10am–1.30pm.*

The "cathedral of cava," dozens of different brands are stocked here by the knowledgeable owner who can discuss the pros and cons of each.

MARKETS

Browsing market stalls holds a fascination for people in search of a bargain, antiques lovers hoping to find that desirable object, or those looking for a gift to take home. There are markets specializing in antiques, arts and crafts, vintage clothing, gourmet foods, and flowers and plants. The earlier you arrive, the greater the choice.

La Boqueria/Mercat de Sant Josep

Ⓜ *Liceu. La Rambla 91. www.boqueria.info. Open Mon–Sat 8am–8.30pm.*

A key stop for any visit to Barcelona, this traditional food market is colorful, bustling, and vibrant. Wander around the elaborately arranged stalls, which sell everything from oranges to razor clams, then sample some of the freshest tapas you'll find in the city at one of the snack counters. It's an architectural treat, too, with a wonderful 19C iron frame topped off by a beautiful glass roof.

♿ Els Encants Vells

Ⓜ *Glòries. Pl. Glòries Catalanes 8. 93 246 30 30. www.encantsbcn. com. Open Apr–Oct Mon, Wed, Fri, Sat 9am–7pm (Nov–Mar 6pm).*

Barcelona's biggest flea market—there are around 500 traders—is also known as Mercat Fira de Bellcaire ("the old charms fair"). A handful of stalls with cheap, new goods—clothes, cleaning materials—is combined with enough bric-a-brac to satisfy the most avid junk-hunter—everything from vintage light fittings to old furniture and architectural salvage. Get there early and be ready to bargain hard.

Fira de Nautumismo

Ⓜ *Liceu. Pl. Reial. Open Sun 10am–2.30pm.*

The majority of stalls in this little market cater for serious collectors, with displays of coins and stamps. There's a sprinkling of more diverse junk and bric-a-brac, though, so it can be a surprisingly engrossing place to browse.

La Boqueria

©Turespaña

Fira de Santa Llúcia

Ⓜ *Jaume 1. Pl. de la Seu. www.firesifestes.com. Open Dec 1–24 10am–9pm (dates and hours may vary slightly year to year).*

A seasonal Christmas market, and a must if you're in Barcelona at the right time of year. Brightly lit stalls sell a range of ornaments and craftwork, but pride of place goes to the traditional clay nativity scenes with numerous beautifully made—and costly—little figures. Keep an eye open for *cagnares*, funny squatting characters that form a surprising and wholly Catalan addition to the nativity scene.

Mercat de Sant Antoni

Ⓜ *Sant Antoni. C. del Comte d'Urgell 1. 93 423 42 87. www.mercatsbcn.com. Open Mon, Tue, Wed, Thur, Sat 7am–2.30pm, 5–8.30pm, Fri 7am–8.30pm.*

Another fabulous example of industrial architecture, Sant Antoni was built by Antoni Rovira in the late 19C. Today this food and produce market is even bigger than the Boqueria, yet it attracts rather fewer tourists, so you may find it's a more relaxed choice for a leisurely look around. Most of the market closes down in August.

Mercat de Santa Caterina

Ⓜ *Jaume 1. Av. de Francesc Cambó, 16. www.mercatsantacaterina. net. Open Mon–Sat 8am–8pm.*

Dating from 1848, Santa Caterina food and produce market underwent a complete revamp in 2005 under the renowned architects Enri Miralles and Benedetta Tagliabue. The result, with its strik-

Els Encants Vells

©Greg Gladman/APA Publications

ingly multicolored undulating roof, is a new city landmark. The restaurant and tapas bar, while pricey, are well worth a visit.

Mercat Dominical del Llibre de Sant Antoni

Ⓜ *Sant Antoni. C, del Comte d'Urgell 1. www.mercatsbcn.com. Open Sun 10am–3pm (hours extended at Christmas and New Year).*

This vintage book market is held every Sunday on stalls surrounding the Sant Antoni market. In addition to books, you'll find vinyl records, old Spanish magazines, photographs, postcards, and coins.

Mercat Gòtic de Antiguitats

Ⓜ *Liceu. Pl. Nova. www.mercat gotic.com. Open Sept–Jul Thu 10am–9pm.*

This small but well-stocked flea market is in the Barri Gòtic. Most of the stalls deal in smaller items—antique dolls, old clocks, books, and china and pottery. The market is closed in August, and, in December, is replaced by the traditional Christmas market.

MARKETS

133

RESTAURANTS

Some visitors may find mealtimes in Barcelona start a little later than they are used to: lunch is at around 1.30pm and dinner from 9pm, although restaurants catering for tourists are often more flexible. To tide you over, graze on some tapas or *pintxos (see p 147)*, eaten standing at the bar or in the street—you'll find a list of tapas bars on p 146–7.

€   up to €15   €€€   €39 to €45
€€   €15 to €30   €€€€ over €45

La Rambla

Zentraus

€–€€   Mediterranean
🅼 *Liceu. Rambla del Raval 41. 93 443 80 78 . www.Zentraus.com. Closed Mon evening, Sun.*

A big restaurant, used by the locals as their *cantina*, serving salads, pasta, and burgers. An excellent choice for lunch or takeout.

Casa Lucio

€€   Spanish
🅼 *Sant Antoni. C. de Viladomat 59. 93 424 44 01. Closed 3 weeks in Aug.*

Every day, the owner of Casa Lucio creates different delicious Catalan dishes and one-offs. There's also a tapas bar. A must-try restaurant.

Los Caracoles

Orgànic

€€   Vegetarian/Tapas
🅼 *Liceu. C. de la Junta de Comerç 11 . 93 301 09 02. www.antonia organickitchen.com.*

This is where the local vegetarians congregate. The dining room is vast, with tables arranged around a mouthwatering buffet.

Les Quinze Nits

€€   Mediterranean
🅼 *Liceu. Ptge Madoz 5 . 93 317 30 75. www.lesquinzenits.com.*

A great location overlooking Plaça Reial. The decor is understated and the food both excellent and inexpensive. You can't book and it's very popular, so get there early.

Los Caracoles

€€€   Catalan
🅼 *Drassanes. C. Escudellers 14. 93 301 20 41. www.loscaracoles.es.*

This restaurant has been owned and run by the same family since 1835 and is justifiably famous. Traditional Catalan cuisine.

Casa Leopoldo

€€€€   Mediterranean
🅼 *Liceu. C. San Rafael 24. 93 441 30 14. www.casaleopoldo.com. Closed Mon, Aug, public holidays.*

R. Mattes/Michelin

Els Quatre Gats

The location is unrefined, the cuisine quite the opposite. Run by the widow of a Portuguese matador, it's a haunt for *corrida* enthusiasts.

Barri Gòtic

Can Culleretes

€€ **Catalan**

Ⓜ *Jaume 1. C. Quintana 5 . 93 317 30 22. www.culleretes.com. Closed Mon except public holidays, Sun evening, Easter Mon, mid-Jul–mid-Aug, Dec 25, 26.*

Founded in 1786, this is Barcelona's oldest restaurant and the second oldest in Spain. The cuisine is classic Catalan and the decor is equally traditional—walls covered in *azulejos*, ceiling hung with hams.

Els Quatre Gats

€€ **Mediterranean**

Ⓜ *Catalunya. C. Montsió 3bis. 93 302 41 40. www.4gats.com.*

An icon of Modernist and bohemian Barcelona *(see p 73)*, this café was the haunt of local artists including Picasso, who designed the menu cover. The style is still the same, and the lunch menu is good value.

El Gran Café

€€–€€€ **Catalan**

Ⓜ *Liceu. C. Avinyó 9. 93 318 79 86. www.restaurantelgrancafe.com.*

A charming, traditional-style restaurant serving Catalan dishes to match. The ambience is good, with live piano music in the evenings.

Opaqo

€€–€€€ **Catalan**

Ⓜ *Jaume I. C. Ciutat 10 . 93 318 46 76 . www.restaurantopaqo.com. Closed Sat lunchtime and Sun.*

This little restaurant, with its simple decor, is known for its creative Mediterranean cuisine. The "surprise" tasting menu is good value and half portions are available.

El Pintor

€€–€€€ **Catalan**

Ⓜ *Jaume I. C. Sant Honorat 7. 93 301 40 65. www.gruptravi.com/pintor.*

Plenty of variety and Catalan flavors in a rustic setting of exposed beams and walls of bare brick and stone—the building was once a painter's workshop. Very pleasant.

La Ribera

Mar de la Ribera

€€ **Spanish**

🅜 *Jaume 1. C. Sombrerers 7. 93 315 13 36. Closed Mon lunchtime, Sun, 2 weeks in Aug.*

Right beside Santa Maria del Mar, this little restaurant serves delectable seafood, paella, and *chipirones* (little squid), always with a smile.

El Nou Celler

€€ **Catalan/Mediterranean**

🅜 *Jaume 1. C. Princesa 16. 93 310 47 73. Closed Sat and Sun evening.*

An unpretentious tavern offering non-stop, friendly service and plenty of atmosphere. The dishes of the day are copious and delicious (the *pulpitos* are to die for).

Seynor Parellada

€€ **Catalan/Mediterranean**

🅜 *Jaume 1. C. Argenteria 35. 93 310 50 94. www.seynorparellada. com. Closed Dec 25.*

Try this elegant establishment, decorated in cheerful blue and yellow, for its refined and inexpensive Catalan cuisine.

Ávalon

€€–€€€ **Catalan/ Mediterranean**

🅜 *Jaume 1. Pare Gallifa 3. 93 295 79 05. www.grandhotelcentral.com.*

An informal setting in the Grand Hotel Central. Catalan cuisine with a homemade country feel, but don't be fooled—the menu was masterminded by a chef with two Michelin stars.

Bar del Pla

€€€ **Mediterranean**

🅜 *Jaume 1. C. Montcada 2 . 93 268 30 03. www.pla-repla.com. Closed Mon.*

The imaginative food conjured up by this branch of the Pla restaurant attracts lots of local diners. The menu changes daily.

El Yantar de la Ribera

€€€ **Castilian**

🅜 *Tetuan. Roger de Flor 114. 93 265 63 09. www.elyantardela ribera.com. Closed Sun evening.*

The decor in all the dining areas here is traditional, as is the menu. Meat roasted to perfection in wood-fired ovens is the house specialty. Takeout is also available.

Flash Flash

7 Portes

€€€ **Catalan**

Ⓜ *Barceloneta. Pg d'Isabel II. 93 319 30 33. www.7portes.com.*

This chic restaurant, under the porticos of Porxos d'En Xifré, opened in 1836. *Arroses* (rice-based dishes and paella) are the house specialty. Impeccable service.

Comerç 24

€€€€ **Tapas**

Ⓜ *Arc de Triomf. C. Comerç 24. 93 319 21 02. www.comerc24.com. Closed Mon, last 3 weeks in Aug, Christmas week.*

The cuisine here can only be described as tapas with attitude—the owner, a disciple of Ferran Adrià, takes the basic concept and raises it to gourmet level, in a classic restaurant environment.

L'Eixample

Alba Granados

€€ **Spanish**

Ⓜ *Lesseps. C. Enric Granados 34. 93 454 61 16. www.albagranados.com.*

Stylish and creative Spanish cuisine, with a specialty of meat cooked on a stone grill. Private dining rooms available for groups.

Flash Flash

€€ **Tortilla**

Ⓜ *Metro. C. La Granada del Penedès 25. 93 237 09 90. www.flashflash.com.*

This *tortilliería* is not only popular and very chic, it's also inexpensive and the range of tortillas on offer is stunning—around 70 variations.

Alan Moore/Michelin
La Polpa

La Polpa

€€ **Mediterranean**

Ⓜ *Lesseps. C. Enric Granados 69. 93 323 83 08. www.lapolpa-restaurant.com. Closed Dec 25, 26.*

A very good value for money menu served in attractive, fresh, white surroundings—it's like eating in a farmhouse kitchen.

La Vinateria de Verdi

€€ **Spanish**

Ⓜ *Lesseps. C. Verdi 138. 93 415 39 96.*

This wine bar, decorated with photos of its illustrious patrons, serves food from Navarre. It also hosts regular "gastronomic weeks ."

La Cúpula

€€–€€€ **Mediterranean**

Ⓜ *Sagrada Familia. C. Sicilia 255. 93 208 20 61. www.lacupula restaurant.com. Closed Mon, Sun.*

There's plenty to catch your eye here, including cars dating from the 1920s and some interesting artworks. The food is also stylishly presented and very good value.

RESTAURANTS

137

Cinc Sentis
©Cinc Sentis

Cal Xim

€€€ **Catalan**

 Verdaguer. C. de Girona 145 .
93 459 20 30 . www.calxim.com/
BCN. Closed Sat, Sun, Easter week,
2 weeks in Aug.

The ambience is contemporary and
the staff are welcoming here. The
menu comprises traditional cuisine
and chargrilled meats, and there's
an excellent wine cellar.

Can Ravell

€€€ **Spanish/Tapas**

Ⓜ Girona. C. Arago 313. 93 457 51
14. www.ravell.com. Closed Mon,
Sun evening.

Attached to a delicatessen, this
restaurant serves a diverse range,
from Catalan classics and tapas to
hamburgers of considerable proportions, to be shared with friends.

Taktika Berri

€€€ **New Spanish**

Ⓜ Hospital Clinic. C. València 169.
93 453 47 59 . Closed Sat evening,
Sun, public holidays, 3 weeks in Aug.

High-quality Basque cuisine served
in an elegant dining room, where
the delightful owners tend to their
equally devoted clientele. Booking
is essential, as far ahead as possible.

Alkimia

€€€€ **New Spanish**

Ⓜ Sagrada Família. C. Industria
79. 93 207 61 15. www.alkimia.cat.
Closed Sat, Sun, 5 days in Easter
week, 3 weeks in Aug.

Traditional Spanish cuisine brought
into the 21C, exquisitely presented in
elegant, understated surroundings.
If you can't decide what to choose,
opt for the tasting menu.

Cinc Sentis

€€€€ **Catalan**

Ⓜ Universitat. Aribau 58. 93 207
61 15. www.cincsentits.com. Closed
Sun, Easter week, last 3 weeks in Aug.

Innovative dishes made from top-
quality local ingredients. Choose
from one of two tasting menus,
either six or eight courses.

Drolma

€€€€ **Catalan**

Ⓜ Diagonal. Pg de Gracia 70. 93
496 77 10. www.drolmarestaurant.
cat. Closed Sun.

Elegant dining in the Hotel Majestic's one-Michelin-star restaurant.
You can choose from the prestige
menu or the slightly less expensive
market menu—the freshest seasonal ingredients are used for both.

Saüc

€€€€ **Catalan**

Ⓜ Hospital Clinic. Ptge Lluís
Pellicer 12. 93 321 01 89. www.sauc
restaurant.com. Closed Mon, Sun,
1 week in Jan, 3 weeks in Aug.

A modern take on traditional
Catalan with some avant-garde in-
gredient combinations, so prepare
to be adventurous but impressed.

Waterfront

Andy-Café

€€   **Mediterranean**
Ⓜ *Poblenou. Av. Diagonal
161–163, 93 486 88 00.
www.amrey-hotels.com.*

In the Poblenou district, and
convenient for Bogatell beach, this
modern café in the Hotel Amrey
Diagonal serves light, healthy food.

Agut

€€–€€€ **Catalan**
Ⓜ *Jaume I. C. d'en Gignàs, 16.
93 315 17 09. Closed Mon, Sun
evening, Aug.*

This restaurant has been serving
Catalan specialties since 1924, in a
huge vaulted dining room oozing
charm. Excellent value lunch menu.

Can Solé

€€€   **Catalan**
Ⓜ *Barceloneta. C. Sant Carles 4. 93
221 50 12. www.cansole.cat. Closed
Mon, Sun evening, 2 weeks in Aug.*

An excellent eatery known for its
seafood and rice dishes, with pretty
decor in shades of blue and photographs of famous clients.

Elx

€€€   **Spanish**
Ⓜ *Barceloneta. Maremagnum,
Moll d'Espanya 5. 93 225 81 17.
www.restaurantelx.com.*

The sister of Elche in Montjuïc, Elx
boasts a romantic setting by the
sea. The Levantine cuisine focuses
on rice dishes, seafood, and salads.

Lluçanès

€€€€ **Mediterranean**
Ⓜ *Barceloneta. Pl. de la Font.
93 224 25 25. www.restaurant
llucanes.com. Closed Mon, Sun
evening, Jan 1, Dec 25, Dec 24
evening, Dec 31 evening.*

Mediterranean cuisine with Asian
influences, served in a light, airy,
interesting building. Choose from
the seasonal or à la carte menus.

Els Pescadors

€€€€ **Seafood**
Ⓜ *Poblenou. Pl. Prim 1. 93 225
20 18. www.elspescadors.com.
Closed Jan 1, Easter, Dec 24–26, 31.*

This restaurant has three dining
areas, one converted from a traditional tavern, and a terrace for summer dining. Menu changes daily.

Drolma

©Majestic Hotel Group

Montjuïc

Elche

€€€ **Spanish**
Ⓜ *Paral·lel. C. Vilà Vilà 71. 93 441 30 89. www.restaurantelche.com.*

This family-run restaurant was established in 1959 in the area below Montjuïc. The owers have become famous for their rice dishes from the Levante, including a selection of paellas.

Pedralbes

L'Arrosseria Xàtiva

€€–€€€ **Mediterranean**
Ⓜ *Entença. C. Bordeus 35. 93 322 65 31. www.arrosseriaxativa.com. Closed Sun evening and public holiday evenings.*

A cozy restaurant serving a selection of Valencian rice dishes. You can eat "cullereta"-style—straight from the pan with a wooden spoon. The lunchtime menu is excellent value and takeout is also available.

La Tertúlia

€€€ **Catalan**
Ⓜ *Entença. C. Morales 15. 93 419 58 97. www.arrosseriaxativa.com. Closed Sun evening and public holiday evenings.*

A very attractive restaurant and in summer you can eat outside on the terrace. The Catalan-based cuisine is beautifully presented and there's live music on Friday and Saturday evenings.

Neichel

€€€€ **Mediterranean**
Ⓜ *Maria Cristina. C. Beltrán I Rózpide 1. 93 203 84 08. www.neichel.es. Closed Mon, Sun, public holidays, 1st week in Jan, last 3 weeks in Aug.*

This restaurant, which holds an award for its interior design and overlooks a garden, is located in the Hotel AC Victoria Suites. Menu options include a "petit" menu, a tasting menu, and and an extensive prestige menu which allows you to enjoy a wider range of dishes.

Paella at L'Arrosseria Xàtiva

©Fernanda Porto/L'Arrosseria Xàtiva

Tibidabo

El Asador de Aranda

€€€   **Catalan**
Tram Blau to stop 31. Av. de Tibidabo 31. 93 417 01 15. www.asadordearanda.com.

An excellent restaurant housed in a strikingly colorful Art Nouveau building. The specialty is tender lamb, slow-cooked in a clay oven.

FURTHER AFIELD

Figueres

El Café del Barri Vell

€   **Mediterranean**
Pl. de les Patates 7, Figueres. 97 250 57 76.

Vegetarian dishes, salads, and light meals served in a pleasant environment—good for a lunch stop.

Mas Pau

€€€€   **Mediterranean**
Avinyolet de Puigventós 17742, Figueres. 97 254 61 54. www.maspau.com. Closed Mon, Tue lunchtime year round, Sun evening Sept–Jun.

An elegant but traditional restaurant in a restored 16C farmhouse. serving stylish and innovative dishes.

Girona

Le Bistrot

€   **Mediterranean**
C. Pujada Sant Domènech 4, Girona. 97 221 88 03.

This lively, popular bistro is in a great location and particularly good for warm summer evenings.

El Asador de Aranda

Alan Moore/Michelin

El Pati Verd

€€€   **Mediterranean**
Pl. Miquel Santaló, Girona. 97 221 12 12. www.carlemany.es. Closed Sun, some public holidays.

Dine in a beautiful conservatory surrounded by lush greenery. Weekday lunch menu available, as well as seasonal menus and "theme" days.

Sitges

El Rincón de Pepe

€€€   **Catalan**
Pg de la Ribera 35, Sitges. 93 894 50 54. www.hotelsitges.com.

A bright dining area with colorful artworks and a terrace overlooking the sea. They specialize in locally-caught fish dishes and stews.

La Santa Maria

€€–€€€   **Mediterranean**
Paseo de la Ribera 52, Sitges. 93 894 09 99. www.lasantamaria.com.

A good value for money restaurant renowned for its seafood, with several traditional-style dining rooms and a terrace facing the sea.

RESTAURANTS

COOL FOR KIDS

Some kids are adventurous with new cuisines and others simply are not, so here is a selection of restaurants serving dishes that will appeal to most children, at a reasonable price. Some have thoughtfully provided ways to keep young children entertained, such as a toy box, a drawing competition, or even a magician. If your child has a birthday while you're on holiday, several restaurants will organize a party in a private room.

Bar del Convent

Ⓜ *Jaume I. Pl. del Convent. 93 256 50 17. www.bardelconvent.com. Closed Sun.*

Home-made pasta and rice dishes, salads, and cakes. There's a drawing table and a toy box to keep the kids amused.

La Bella Napoli

Ⓜ *Poble Sec. C. de Margarit 12. 93 442 50 56. www.bellanapoli.net.*

Great pizza, pasta, and risotto is served here, so the grown-ups will love it too. It's very popular so it's best to book.

BIOasis

Ⓜ *Catalunya. C. Bonsuccés 8. 93 304 15 59.*

A small, family-run restaurant serving vegetarian food at very reasonable prices. Kids are provided with drawing paper and pens.

El Bosc de les Fades

Ⓜ *Drassanes. Ptge de la Banca 5 . 93 317 26 49 . www.museucerabcn.com.*

Adjoining the Waxworks Museum, an enchanted forest/kitsch bar where you can have a drink and shelter from the storm…

Fish and Chips Barcelona

Ⓜ *Liceu. Rambla del Raval 26. 93 441 11 34. www.fishandchips barcelona.com.*

Traditional British fare—fish, steak and kidney pies, and sausages, all served with chipped potatoes.

Fresc Co

MUST EAT

Foster's Hollywood American Restaurant

Ⓜ *Pg de Gràcia. C. Balmes 76. 93 496 03 87 www.fostershollywood.es. Branches at 2 other locations.*

American and Mexican cuisine. A magician is on hand to provide entertainment on Saturday and Sunday afternoons.

Fresc Co

Ⓜ *Fontana. Gran de Gràcia 30 . 93 301 68 37. www.fresco.com. Branches at 15 other locations.*

A fixed-price buffet with fresh, delicious, Mediterranean dishes in a contemporary environment.

Hard Rock Cafe

Ⓜ *Catalunya. Pl. Catalunya 21. 93 270 23 05. www.hardrock.com.*

American and Tex-Mex food amid Rock 'n' Roll memorabilia, in a lively atmosphere. There's a private room for children's parties.

Els Pescadors

Ⓜ *Poblenou. Pl. Prim 1. 93 225 20 18. www.elspescadors.com. Closed Jan 1, Easter, Dec 24–26, 31.*

Unusually for a gourmet restaurant, Els Pescadors has a special kids' menu. The choices will be familiar but the quality exceptional.

Pizza Marzano

Ⓜ *Catalunya. Rambla Canaletes 140. 93 342 70 51. www.pizza marzano.com. 4 other branches.*

The first in this chain of pizzerias was opened in the city in 2001. The kids' menu includes a pizza or a pasta dish, a dessert, and a drink.

Alan Moore/Michelin

El Racó

Els Pollos de llull

Branches at C. Napols 272, Ramon Turro 13, Sant Roc 24. 607 350 289. www.elspollos.com.

Roast chicken is the theme here. There's an excellent value lunch menu Mon–Fri, and a chicken-drawing competition for fun.

El Racóa

Branches at Corsega 196, Rambla Catalunya 25, Pl. Urquinaona 7, and Ronda Universitat 11. www.elraco.com.

Mediterranean cuisine, with plenty of choice for all tastes—pizza, quizza, pasta, rice dishes, steaks, and pancakes.

Semproniana

Ⓜ *Diagonal. C. Rosselló 148. 93 453 18 20. www.semproniana.net.*

An elegant restaurant serving traditional Catalan cuisine, but they have a fun attitude to kids' food, such as offering the kids' menu at the price of your child's age (Mon–Thu).

CAFÉS

Barcelona has plenty of cafés where you can do as the city's intellectuals and artists have been doing for decades—sit and relax with a cup of coffee, chat, and simply watch the world go by. Barcelona also has a great selection of *xocolatiers*—cafés specializing in the thickest, most delicious hot chocolate, to be enjoyed with a pastry.

Buenas Migas

Ⓜ *Diagonal. Pg de Gràcia 120. 92 238 55 49. www.buenasmigas. com. Branches in 7 other locations.*

A growing chain of really attractive, informal cafés where the house specialty is foccaccia served with delicious toppings. Genovese fishermen would eat a piece of foccaccia before venturing out to sea. Pasta and salads are also available. Open for breakfast through to dinner.

Café de l'Opera

Ⓜ *Liceu. Rambla 74 . 93 317 75 85 . www.cafeoperabcn.com.*

This historic café opposite the Gran Teatre del Liceu, with its Modernist façade and 19C feel, is a veritable Barcelona institution. The menu includes everything from

coffee and cakes to ice cream, beer, tapas, wine, cognac, and delicious chocolates.

🍴 Café Zurich

Ⓜ *Catalunya. Pl. de Catalunya 1. 93 317 91 53.*

Your stay in Barcelona must include at least one visit to this café, which has been in business for over a hundred years. The prices are a little on the high side, but you can't beat the location—the perfect spot for people watching.

Dulcinea

Ⓜ *Liceu. C. de Petritxol 2. 93 302 86 24.*

This traditional *xocolateria*, founded in 1803, is one of the city's oldest, famed for its *melindros* to accompany hot chocolate.

Buenas Migas

Escribà

🅜 *Liceu. Rambla de les Flors 83. 93 301 60 27. www.escriba.es. Branches in 2 other locations.*

A renowned family establishment housed in an old building painstakingly refurbished in Modernist style in 1902. A perfect pit stop.

Fargas

🅜 *Liceu. C. del Pi 16. 93 320 03 42.*

Famous in Barcelona, this old-fashioned *xocolatier* was opened in 1937 and has a city council plaque to mark its years of service.

Gelateria Xocolateria Santa Clara

🅜 *Jaume 1. C. de la Llibreteria 2. 93 315 12 57.*

If the prospect of both ice cream and hot chocolate under one roof is your idea of heaven, then head to the Plaça de Sant Jaume, where this little café is tucked away.

El Jardí

🅜 *Liceu. C. Hospital 56. 93 329 15 50. www.eljardibarcelona.es.*

This remarkably peaceful spot in the courtyard of the Antic Hospital de Sant Pau is a great place for breakfast, lunch, tapas, and everything between. You might even catch some live music.

Mesón del Café

🅜 *Jaume I. C. Llibreteria 16. 93 315 07 54.*

A tiny traditional coffee bar in the Barri Gòtic, opened in 1909. The coffee here is really special, so it's often very crowded.

Escribà

R. Mattés/Michelin

Nakupenda

🅜 *Barceloneta. Av. Marqués de Argentera 7. 93 268 04 35. www.nakupenda.com.*

There's nothing traditional about this avant-garde establishment in El Born, which specializes in soups and smoothies. Nutrition is high on the agenda.

Venus Delicatessen

🅜 *Jaume I. C. Avinyó 25. 93 301 11 58.*

Not a delicatessen, in spite of the name, but simply a café serving inexpensive light meals all day, as well as coffee and cakes.

Xocoa

🅜 *Catalunya. C. Petritxol 11. 93 301 11 97. www.xocoa-bcn.com.*

You could probably spend an entire day in this trendy café, attached to one of Xocoa's chain of shops, starting with breakfast— and hot chocolate, of course.

CAFÉS

TAPAS BARS

Originating in Andalucia, southern Spain, the word "tapa" means "cover," and it is thought the name derives from the practice of placing a slice of salami or ham on a glass of wine to keep out the dust and flies. Today we know tapas as small portions of food commonly served as a snack before lunch or dinner—as simple as a bowl of olives or more filling dishes such as spicy fried potatoes, slices of cured ham, or seafood in tomato sauce.

Bar Mundial

Arc de Triomf. Pl. St Agustí Vell 1. 93 319 90 56.

Founded in 1925, this popular family-run bar is always full-to-bursting. And with good reason, the portions are generous and the seafood (shrimp, octopus, shellfish) are fresh and tasty. If you prefer to sit down at a table, it's best to book ahead.

Cal Pep

M *Barceloneta/Jaume 1. Pl. de les Olles 8. 93 310 79 61. www.calpep.com.*

Delicious tapas served in a busy, noisy bar. Grab a counter seat if you can and try the fabulous artichokes, cured hams, sausages, or seafood. You might even meet Pep himself as he does his rounds to check you are enjoying his dishes.

Celta

M *Drassanes. C. de la Mercè 16. 93 315 00 06.*

One of this street's best tapas bars, where, as you stand at the counter, you face displays overflowing with tapas: croquettes, *patatas bravas, pulpo a la gallega…* all the Galician classics are here, waiting to be tasted with the traditional cider.

Euskal Etxea

M *Liceu. Pl. Montcada 1–3. 93 310 21 85. euskaletxeak.org.*

A tapas/*pintxos* bar near the church of Santa Maria del Mar.

Taller de Tapas

©Greg Gladman/APA Publications

Choose from the counter at the front or the tables at the back to taste the *pintxos* or the excellent Basque-style tapas.

Irati

🅜 *Liceu Cardenal Casanyes 17. 93 302 3084.*

A typical Basque tavern, close to the Teatre del Liceu. Some of the dishes are cooked on the barbecue.

Navarra

🅜 *Pg de Gràcia. Pg de Gràcia 4. 93 318 58 95.*

Great location, great food. This tapas bar in Passeig de Gràcia brings together the modern and the traditional in decor with dishes from Navarra, the Basque region, and Catalunya. Sit at the long bar and enjoy the ambience and the delicious food.

Taller de Tapas

🅜 *Liceu. Pl. Sant Josep Oriol 9. 93 301 80 20. www.tallerdetapas.com.*

Visitors often find tapas bars a bit daunting because ordering at the counter can prove a challenge, so this is a good compromise: comfortably seated in the dining room

or on the terrace, you can choose your tapas from the menu and they will be brought to you.

Tapa Tapa

🅜 *Pg de Gràcia. Pg de Gràcia 44. 93 488 33 69.*

Similar to Taller de Tapas, an adaptation of the tapas bar for sightseers with tired legs! Offers a vast choice of good dishes, and the price depends on how hungry you are.

Taverna del Born

🅜 *Barceloneta. Pg del Born 27–9. 93 315 09 64.*

Prop up the bar and enjoy the lively ambience while tasting the house-special tapas: cod, croquettes, langoustines with mushrooms, all accompanied by the traditional *pa amb tomàquet* (tomato-soaked bread).

El Xampanyet

🅜 *Jaume I. Carrer Montcada 22. 93 319 70 03.*

Opened in 1929, and highly recommended ever since, this *azulejos*-clad café serves draft cider and cava with its excellent tapas. Its anchovies are famous in Barcelona!

TAPAS BARS

147

HOTELS

Barcelona has a great choice of accommodations, from simple *pensións* to the most sumptuous hotels, in styles ranging from traditional to cutting-edge modern. The establishments listed below were selected for their ambience, location, and/or value for money. Prices reflect the average cost for a standard double room for two people in high season. Breakfast is not usually included. Advance booking is essential and can get you some great deals.

€	under €50	€€€	€75 to €120
€€	€50 to €75	€€€€	over €120

La Rambla

Hotel Condal

€   **53 rooms**
Ⓜ *Liceu. C. Boqueria 23. 93 318 18 82. www.hotelcondal.es.*

Opened in 1850, this is one of Barcelona's oldest hotels. It was refurbished in 2000 to provide a modern interior behind the original façade. The hotel has its own café-bar.

Hostal Gat Xino

€€   **34 rooms**
Ⓜ *Liceu. C. Hospital 155. 93 324 88 33. www.gatrooms.es.*

A central location, fresh, contemporary decor in white with flashes of lime green, and a roof terrace for relaxing. Breakfast is included.

Hosteria Grau

€€   **18 rooms**
Ⓜ *Catalunya. C. Ramelleres 27. 93 301 81 35. www.hostalgrau.com.*

This *pensión* offers simple Catalan decor, with plain tiled floors. Self-catering apartments are also available here. Check out the Bar Centric next door—it has an interesting history.

Hotel Peninsular

€€   **80 rooms**
Ⓜ *Liceu. C. San Pau 34. 93 302 31 38. www.hotelpeninsular.net.*

The rooms here occupy the cells of a former Augustinian convent and although they retain a rather austere feel, they are fresh and clean.

Hotel Roma Reial

€€   **52 rooms**
Ⓜ *Liceu. Pl. Reial 11. www.hotel romareial.com.*

Not the most exciting decor but a really lovely location. The dining room in the basement is interesting, with the original stone arches.

Hotel Casa Camper

€€€   **25 rooms**
Ⓜ *Catalunya. C. Elisabets 11. 93 342 62 80. www.casacamper.com.*

This unique boutique hotel, housed in a 19C tenement building, offers minimalist decor without compromising on comfort. Asian food is served tapas-style in the restaurant.

Hotel Catalonia Duques de Bergara

€€€   149 rooms

🅼 *Catalunya. C. Bergara11. 93 301 51 51. www.duques.barcelona hotels.it.*

The modern, functional accommodation is housed in a striking, recently restored building designed by Gaudí's tutor, the Modernist architect Emilio Salas (1899).

Hotel Gaudí

€€€   73 rooms

🅼 *Liceu. Nou de la Rambla 12. 93 317 90 32. www.hotelgaudi barcelona.com.*

In a great location right opposite the Palau Güell, this Gaudí-inspired hotel is fresh and modern. The accommodation options include quadruple rooms for families.

Hotel Husa Oriente

€€€   142 rooms

🅼 *Liceu. C. La Rambla 45. 93 302 25 58. www.husa.es/Oriente.*

This hotel occupies a former convent building. Choose a room overlooking lively La Rambla (soundproof windows help block out the bustle) or the peaceful convent cloister.

Hotel Mesón Castilla

€€€   56 rooms

🅼 *Liceu. C. de Valdoncella 5. 93 318 21 82. www.mesoncastilla.com.*

Prices are at the higher end of this category but the location is good and in certain months the hotel offers 5 nights for the price of 4.

Hotel Pulitzer

€€€   91 rooms

🅼 *Catalunya. C. Bergara 8. 93 481 67 67. www.hotelpulitzer.es.*

Light, airy, and avant garde, this hotel is so beautifully designed you might feel tempted to forget the sightseeing and just relax on the rooftop patio.

Olivia Plaza Hotel

€€€€   113 rooms

🅼 *Catalunya. Pl. Catalunya19. 93 316 87 00. www.oliviahotels.es.*

Opened in 2006, this hotel offers modern and stylish accommodation in an excellent central location. The cuisine in the hotel's Nineteen restaurant is equally modern.

Olivia Plaza Hotel

©Olivia Plaza Hotel

HOTELS

Barri Gòtic

Hotel Call

€ **23 rooms**
Ⓜ *Liceu. Arc. Sant Ramo del Call 4.
93 302 11 23. www.hotelcall.net.*

An attractive, functional, and
well-maintained hotel in a great
location. The rooms are clean and
bright, and you get a good deal for
this category of hotel.

Hostal Coral

€ **25 rooms**
Ⓜ *Jaume I. C. Calella 1. 93 317
68 41. www.hostalcoral.com*

Opened in 2005, Hostal Coral is
centrally located in a quiet square
behind the Plaça Sant Jaume. It's
all very modern and spotlessly
clean.

Hostal Sol y K

€ **14 rooms**
Ⓜ *Liceu. C. Cervantes 2.
93 318 81 48. www.solyk.com.*

One of the rare central hotels
that's both affordable and stylish.
Contemporary and light, each
room is unique and tastefully
decorated.

El Jardí

€€ **40 rooms**
Ⓜ *Liceu. Pl. Sant Josep Oriol 1.
93 301 59 00. www.hoteljardi
barcelona.com.*

Ask for a room with a balcony
overlooking the square if you want
to soak up the atmosphere from
above. The hotel has been completely remodeled and the rooms
are spacious, fresh and modern.

Catalonia Albinoni

€€€ **74 rooms**
Ⓜ *Catalunya. Portal de l'Angel 17.
93 318 41 41. www.hoteles-
catalonia.com.*

This stylish hotel occupies a beautiful mansion dating from 1876 but
the rooms are contemporary and
elegant in style. The terrace rooms
open out to the garden.

Hotel Cortès

€€€ **44 rooms**
Ⓜ *Catalunya. C. de Santa Anna 25.
93 317 92 12. www.hotelcortes.com.*

Comfortable, functional, no-frills
accommodation and good value
for money in an ideal location.

View from El Jardí hotel

©Hotel el Jardí

Hostal Sol y K

©Hostal Sol y K

Hotel Colón

€€€ **141 rooms**
Ⓜ *Jaume I. Av. Catedral 7. 93 301 14 04. www.hotelcolon.es.*

This attractive hotel, which opened in 1951, is in an excellent location overlooking the cathedral. Choose to stay here and you will join an impressive list of former guests.

Hotel Neri

€€€€ **22 rooms**
Ⓜ *Liceu. Sant Sever 5. 93 304 06 55. www.hotelneri.com.*

Housed in a small 18C palace, the rooms in this hotel, designed by artists, are quirky and interesting. In the restaurant, classic regional cuisine is presented in modern style.

La Ribera

Pensión Ciudadela

€ **10 rooms**
Ⓜ *Jaume I. C. del Comerç. 93 319 62 03. www.pension-ciudadela.com.*

The rooms in this simple guesthouse, though somewhat austere, are clean and a good size. It's a very reasonably priced *pensión* and well situated for sightseeing.

Pensión Francia

€ **11 rooms**
Ⓜ *Barceloneta. C. Rera Palau 4. 93 319 03 76.*

This welcoming family-run guest- house is at the top of an old building, so be prepared for a climb. The rooms are clean, spacious, and simply decorated.

Hotel Banys Orientals

€€ **43 rooms**
Ⓜ *Jaume I. C. Argenteria 37. 93 268 84 60. www.hotelbanys orientals.com.*

Extremely attractive rooms in a lovely old building. The hotel's elegant suites are housed in two separate buildings nearby.

chic&basic

€€€ **31 rooms**
Ⓜ *Jaume I, Arc de Triomf. C. Princesa 50. 93 295 46 52. www.chicandbasic.com.*

HOTELS

chic&basic

©chic&basic

This hotel is not as basic (or as cheap) as the name might imply, but chic it definitely is. The food served up in the White Bar is as intriguing as the hotel's decor.

L'Eixample

Hostal Central

€ **16 rooms**
Ⓜ *Universitat. Ronda Universitat 11. 93 302 24 20. www.hostal central.net.*

A small and comfortable guesthouse with fresh and attractive rooms. The room prices are very reasonable, and even more so if you don't mind sharing a bathroom.

Pensión Norma

€ **18 rooms**
Ⓜ *Fontana. C. Gran de Gràcia 87. 93 237 44 78.*

This simple but bright little guesthouse comes highly recommended. It's laid out over two floors (no elevator) and has pleasant little communal terraces with rooftop views. Wifi is available.

Hotel Ginebra

€€ **11 rooms**
Ⓜ *Catalunya. Rambla de Catalunya 1. 93 317 10 63. www.hotelginebra.net.*

This hotel occupies a fine old town house (1880) in a great location, with impeccably maintained rooms and lovely views.

Hostal Goya/Goya Principal

€€ **19 rooms**
Ⓜ *Catalunya. Pau Claris 74. 93 302 25 65. www.hostalgoya.com.*

There is a home-from-home atmosphere here, with friendly,

©Hostal Goya

Hostal Goya Principal

helpful staff. The two sections of the hostel offer a choice of modern or more traditional accommodation.

Hotel Lleó

€€ **89 rooms**
Ⓜ *Catalunya. C. Pelai 22–4. 93 318 13 12. www.hotel-lleo.com.*

Some rooms have very modern decor, others are more traditional in this comfortable, value-for-money hotel.

Hotel Gran Ducat

€€–€€€ **64 rooms**
Ⓜ *Urquinaona. Ronda Sant Pere 15. 93 342 63 70. www.hotelgran ducat.com.*

A beautiful building in a central location. The hotel opened in 2001 and the interior is bright and modern behind the carefully preserved façade.

Hotel Acta Atrium Palace

€€€ **71 rooms**
Ⓜ *Catalunya. Gran Via de les Corts Catalanes 656. 93 255 30 00. www.hotel-atriumpalace.com.*

This hotel conceals a bright, updated interior hidden behind its late-19C façade. Temporary art exhibtions are held in the restaurant, which offers Mediterranean cuisine.

Hotel Avenida Palace

€€€ **151 rooms**
Ⓜ *Pg de Gràcia. Gran Via de les Corts Catalanes 605. 93 301 96 00. www.hotelavenidapalace.com.*

Classic elegance is the hallmark of this hotel—it's worth a visit just to admire the grand staircase. The restaurant—Insòlit BCN—serves a lavish buffet for both lunch and dinner in the evening.

Hotel Constanza

€€€ **14 rooms**
Ⓜ *Urquinaona. C. Bruc 33. 93 270 19 10. www.hotelconstanza.com.*

Clean, elegant lines and soothing colors typify the decor in this family-run boutique hotel, which has the advantage of a central but peaceful location.

Hotel Cram

€€€ **67 rooms**
Ⓜ *Universitat. C. d'Aribau, 54. 93 216 77 00. www.hotelcram.com.*

A stylish, cutting-edge hotel with plenty of thoughtful detail, including designer fabrics. The Gaig restaurant holds a Michelin star.

Hotel Praktik Rambla

€€€ **43 rooms**
Ⓜ *Pg de Gràcia. Rambla Catalunya, 27. 93 343 66 90. www.hotel praktikrambla.com.*

A stylish boutique hotel that's not outrageously expensive, with fresh, contemporary decor, a restaurant, and a sun terrace.

Hotel Casa Fuster

€€€€ **96 rooms**
Ⓜ *Diagonal. Pg de Gracia 132. 93 255 30 00. www.barcelona casafusterhotel.com.*

This 5-star hotel is housed in a fine Modernist building. Light, sumptuously decorated rooms and excellent Mediterranean cuisine in the Galaxo Restaurant.

Hotel Majestic

©Majestic Hotel Group

🛏 Hotel Majestic

€€€€   **303 rooms**
Ⓜ *Diagonal. Pg de Gracia 68.*
93 488 17 17. www.hotelmajestic.es.

The influence of Gaudí is much in evidence in this hotel's rooms and suites. Gastronomy is a feature, with a choice of restaurants including the Michelin-starred Drolma.

Hotel Roger de Llúria

€€€€   **48 rooms**
Ⓜ *Urquinaona.*
Roger de Llúria 28. 93 343 60 80.
www.rogerdelluria.com.

This hotel exudes an atmosphere of traditional elegance and comfort. The Mirall restaurant offers Catalan and international cuisines.

Waterfront

Hostel New York

€   **100 beds**
Ⓜ *Drassanes. C. d'en Gignas 6.*
93 315 03 04. www.bcnalberg.com.

There are small dormitories (2–4 beds in each), with shared bathrooms. Bed linen is available to rent (or use a sleeping bag). You'll need a padlock for luggage storage.

Hotel Oasis

€€   **105 rooms**
Ⓜ *Barceloneta. Pl. de Palau 17.*
93 319 43 96. www.hoteloasis
barcelona.com.

Close to the sea but still within easy reach of all the main sights, this attractive family-owned hotel has its own small restaurant.

Pension Segre

€€   **23 rooms**
Ⓜ *Barceloneta. C. Simon Oller 1*
Principal esquina Calle Ample.
93 315 07 09. www.pensionsegre
barcelona.com.

The functional but comfortable accommodation on offer includes a studio apartment (sleeps 6). Some rooms are ensuite.

Hesperia del Mar

€€–€€€   **84 rooms**
Ⓜ *Poblenou. Mare de Déu de*
Bellvitge 3. 93 503 60 52.
www.hesperia.com.

Located close to the waterfront, this hotel is bright and modern. Opt for a room without a sea view to stay in 4-star surroundings at a lower rate.

Montjuïc

Live & Dream

€€€   **13 rooms**
Ⓜ *Mercat Nou. C.*
Rossend Arús 23. 93 332 91 28.
www.liveanddream.com.

A very bright, modern, peaceful, and inexpensive hotel located behind an austere façade. Here, you can hire a bike or car and a takeout lunch.

MUST STAY

B Hotel

€€€ **84 rooms**

 🄼 *Espanya. Gran Via de les Corts Catalanes 389–391. 93 552 95 00. www.b-hotel.com.*

Stylish avant-garde decor in a modern, minimalist hotel. The roof terrace boasts great views.

Pedralbes

Hotel Rey Juan Carlos 1

€€€ **432 rooms**

🄼 *Zona Universitària. Av. Diagonal 661–671. 93 364 40 40. www.hrjuancarlos.com.*

A smart, modern "urban resort" hotel in a delightful setting. Wide range of rooms and suites and some tempting themed packages.

Tibidabo

Gran Hotel La Florida

€€€€ **70 rooms**

Ctra Vallvidrera al Tibidabo 83–93. 93 259 30 00. www.hotel laflorida.com.

Elegant, spacious rooms, gourmet cuisine, and relaxing spa treatments in an exceptional location high above the city.

Figueres

Hotel Travé

€€ **76 rooms**

Ctra Olot s/n. 97 250 06 16. www.hoteltrave.com.

This value-for-money hotel has been recently refurbished in a traditional style. For newlyweds, there's an exceptionally pretty bridal suite.

Hotel Duran

€€ **65 rooms**

C. Lausaca 5. 97 250 12 50. www.hotelduran.com.

With a fresh, contemporary decor, this hotel's award-winning restaurant is a real bonus.

Girona

Pensión Bellmirall

€€ **7 rooms**

C. Bellmirall 3. 97 220 40 09.

Basic accommodation in a charming 14C building in the heart of the medieval city.

Hotel Historic

€€€ **8 rooms, 7 apartments**

C. Bellmirall 4A. 97 222 35 83. www.hotelhistoric.com.

Beams and exposed stone attest to the age of this hotel. The apartments are a great choice for families.

Sitges

La Santa Maria

€€€ **57 rooms**

Paseo de la Ribera 52. 97 894 09 99. www.lasantamaria.com.

This hotel has a perfect location on the seafront. The restaurant serves local and international cuisine.

Hotel Romàntic/ Hotel de la Renaixença

€€–€€€ **78 rooms**

C. Sant Isidre 33. 97 894 83 75. www.hotelromantic.com.

These two charming hotels boast a delightful dining garden, although the interiors are equally attractive.

INDEX

Certain entries, such as architects, artists, churches, cinemas… are listed under **bold** headings. For complete lists of hotels, markets, restaurants, and shops, see the Must Do, Must Eat, and Must Stay sections.

INDEX

List of Maps and Plans

Photo Credits (page Icons)